To Rose and Henry

Student's Vegetarian Cookbook

Quick, Easy, Cheap, and *Tasty* *Vegetarian Recipes*

Carole Raymond

PRIMA PUBLISHING

Published by Prima Publishing, Roseville, California. Member of the Crown Publishing Group, a division of Random House, Inc.

PRIMA PUBLISHING and colophon are trademarks of Random House, Inc., registered with the United States Patent and Trademark Office.

Quote on page xv copyright © 1994 by Andrei Codrescu. *Zombification: Stories from National Public Radio.* Reprinted by permission of St. Martin's Press, Incorporated.

The information for pages xv–xvi was compiled by EarthSave International. Used by permission.

Library of Congress Cataloging-in-Publication Data
Raymond, Carole.
    Student's vegetarian cookbook: quick, easy, cheap, and tasty vegetarian recipes / Carole Raymond.
        p. cm.
    Includes index.
    ISBN 0-7615-0854-6
    1. Vegetarian cookery. 2. Quick and easy cookery. 3. Low-budget cookery. I. Title.
TX837.R3793 1997
641.5'636—dc21   97-8932
                                                                          CIP

02 03 04 05 HH 11 10 9 8

Printed in the United States of America

First Edition

Visit us online at www.primapublishing.com

Contents

Preface

Welcome to vegetarian cooking. There has never been a better time to appreciate the sights, smells, flavors, and textures of a meatless diet.

More and more people are recognizing how vegetarian cooking will benefit their health and please their palate. As markets fill with broader arrays of wholesome foods, even the student or first-time cook can easily turn a basketful of vegetables, grains, and other simple ingredients into delicious, quick, and inexpensive meals. Consider some of the bonuses of vegetarian eating:

- Eating vegetarian means that you can make a great meal with all the necessary nutrients and no meat in just one dish. Pasta, pizza, tacos, quesadillas, fajitas, stir-fries, simple one-pot soups, bread and salad, creamy polenta with mushroom gravy, a bowl of chili, or a baked potato topped with steaming vegetables; all these foods can easily fill the center of any plate.
- For the health conscious, vegetarianism will help you look and feel great. Vegetarian meals are lower in fat than meals that revolve around meat, and recent research suggests that fat calories appear to be the most fattening of all. This may explain why vegetarians are on the average trimmer than their meat-eating counterparts.
- If you like to eat, but don't like cleaning up, vegetarian cooking has another bonus. Without the animal fat that sticks to pans and plates when you cook meat, clean-up is a snap.
- Cultures all over the world center their cuisine on plant foods. As you dip into vegetarian cooking, your plate will fill with the accumulated flavors of many culinary traditions.

If you are just starting out, you may need a helping hand over a few small hurdles. The *Animal Rights Handbook* estimates that the average American will eat 1 calf, 3 lambs, 11 cattle, 23 hogs, 45 turkeys, and 1,097 chickens in a lifetime. You probably grew up thinking of meat as the virtual pillar of the American way of life. The government promoted it, your third grade teacher placed steaks and drumsticks squarely in the middle of the food chart, and television told us meat would make us "real people."

The dominant meat-eating culture is often ignorant about and consequently maligns vegetarians. Here are some of the myths commonly associated with vegetarianism and the facts that dispel them.

- *Vegetarians are weak and frail.* Some of the planet's largest and strongest animals live by eating vegetables—after all, elephants, bulls, gorillas and stallions are all vegetarians. There are many renowned vegetarian athletes, including Dave Scott, one of the greatest triathletes in the world.
- *Vegetarians do not get enough protein.* You can get all the protein you need just by eating a variety of foods every day. The average American diet far exceeds healthy protein requirements.
- *Vegetarians do not get enough calcium.* Research today suggests that dairy products, touted as good sources of calcium, may be calcium inhibitors because of their high protein content. Countries with the highest rates of osteoporosis intake most of their calcium from protein-rich dairy products. If you reduce dairy products in your diet you will get calcium from the same place cows do: from green things that grow in the ground. Lettuce, spinach, and broccoli are all prime sources of calcium.
- *Vegetarians are a tired lot.* If you are looking for more energy, you will get it from eating carbohydrates like potatoes, pasta, and whole grain bread, not from meat.
- *Humans are naturally carnivores.* Human beings are primates whose teeth, intestinal structure, and dietary needs are ideal for eating plant foods, not flesh. (Many believe that eating

meat began during the Ice Age when plant food became scarce.)

- *Health professionals find vegetarian eating a questionable choice.* The Physicians' Committee for Responsible Medicine recently called for four new food groups (whole grains, vegetables, fruits, and legumes) and lists dairy products and meat as optional, not necessary.

Luckily, attitudes are changing. Many people now recognize that a meat-based diet paves the road to many forms of illness, for both humans and the environment. A well-balanced vegetarian diet can provide all the nutrients we need. Many people discover that vegetarian meals surpass their taste expectations. Learning your way out of a meat-eating culture, especially as a beginning cook, can appear daunting.

Vegetarian cooking does not necessarily mean extra hours in the kitchen. No matter how much you love to eat, there are times when you don't feel like squarely facing the stove. Sometimes you need to make life easier by taking advantage of partially prepared and ready-made supermarket foods. Here's a list of 10 quick meals that set aside the sauté pan and instead rely on a can opener and frozen vegetables.

Top 10 List of No-Time-to-Cook Meals

1. *Spaghetti* Boil up a pot of noodles. Open a jar of pasta sauce; heat it in a saucepan with a handful of frozen mixed vegetables. You will be eating in minutes.

2. *Vegetarian soup* Use leftover cooked pasta or rice, and frozen peas to turn a paper cup of packaged soup into a hearty meal.

3. *Salad* Prewashed greens and bottled dressing are a quick fix.

4. *Chili* Open a can of vegetarian chili, and add frozen corn. Heat and serve sprinkled with chopped fresh cilantro.

5. *Tacos* Warm a tortilla on a heated, dry skillet; add canned vegetarian refried beans, lettuce, tomato, and salsa. Fold and eat.

6. *Pizza* Make a gourmet pizza in minutes. Spread a ready-made frozen pizza crust with canned pizza sauce (a 4-ounce can of tomato sauce seasoned with 1 teaspoon dried oregano works beautifully, and it's cheap). Top the sauce with a jar of marinated artichoke hearts, thin onion slices, olives, and bell pepper rings. Scatter feta and mozzarella cheese on top, and bake according to pizza crust directions.

7. *Barbecued Potato* Cut 2 red potatoes into $1/2$-inch cubes. Put them into a microwavable dish with 1 tablespoon of water. Cover. Cook on High in a microwave for about 6 minutes, or until they are tender. Remove the lid, and spoon on several tablespoons of prepared barbecue (or pasta) sauce. Cover, microwave 30 seconds. Remove from oven, sprinkle with Parmesan cheese, and eat.

8. *Baked Potato* Turn a baked potato into a "taco" with canned beans, salsa, and grated cheese, or pour prepared vegetarian soup over the potato for a quick-fix gravy. If you like your potatoes creamy, mix yogurt with tahini and spoon it over the top.

9. *Rice Pilaf* Open a jar of salad dressing and drizzle it over cooked rice sprinkled with seasoned tofu.

10. *Burgers* Buy a box of frozen veggie burgers. Layer a bun with fresh lettuce, tomatoes, and sliced onions. Add your favorite condiments, and enjoy a virtual burger instead of a hamburger.

When you are ready to go beyond fast foods, the *Student's Vegetarian Cookbook* will give you the tools you need to bring a world of fresh and varied tastes onto your table. Grab a cutting board and follow these recipes to good health and great eating!

Acknowledgments

Thanks to everyone who helped my book get published: Susan Silva, Brenda Nichols, Brian Taylor, Jonna Pedrioli, Karen Fraley, Susan Gall, Gloria Tierney, Archetype Book Composition, and James Steinberg.

Thanks also to Richard, Camela, and Jonathan Raymond, Lance Klein, Lisa Klein, Toni Barrientos, Nancy Byles, Roberta Gross, Roberta Miller, Ursula Bacon, and the techs on the Apple help line.

Introduction
"It Bugs Me"

Celebrated author Andrei Codrescu, whose keen observations of American culture can be heard regularly on National Public Radio, has this to say about how eating meat affects the planet, animals, and your health and why building yet another Burger King bugs him:

> *Number one, they kill cows; number two, the cows they kill graze on the sites of murdered forests; number three, the cows they kill that killed the forests are full of hormones; number four, the hormone-filled cows they kill that killed the forests are full of bad-for-your-heart fat; number five, the bad-for-your-heart-hormone-filled-forest-killing-dead-cows are wrapped in bad-for-the-earth-plastic. . . .*

What is a Whopper or Big Mac worth, and are you willing to pay the price? Here are more facts about eating meat that may disturb you:

- Livestock consumes 70% of U.S. grain production. Twenty million people die each year as a result of malnutrition and starvation. Americans could feed 100,000,000 people by reducing their intake of meat by just 10%.
- One acre of prime land can produce many pounds of edible product. Here are a few examples:

  30,000 pounds of apples
  40,000 pounds of potatoes
  50,000 pounds of tomatoes
  250 pounds of beef

- Livestock—cattle, poultry, goats, sheep—totaling 15 billion worldwide now outnumber people three to one. Livestock graze on half of the world's land mass. The explosion of livestock populations has resulted in a parallel explosion of animal wastes that pollute surface and ground water. U.S. livestock produces 230,000 pounds of excrement per second. The amount of waste created by a 10,000-head feed lot is equal to the waste of a city of 110,000 people.

- World livestock production is now a significant factor in the emission of two of the four global warming gasses: carbon dioxide and methane. Every steak we eat has the same effect as a 25-mile drive in a typical American car.
- Each year, an estimated 125,000 square miles of rain forest are permanently destroyed, bringing about the extinction of approximately 1,000 plant and animal species.
- Producing one pound of feedlot steak results in the loss of 35 pounds of topsoil. It takes 200 to 1,000 years to form one inch of topsoil.
- It takes 2,500 gallons of water to produce 1 edible pound of beef. It takes 49 gallons of water to produce 1 edible pound of apples.
- Eighty percent of the meat produced in the United States contains drugs that are passed on to you when you eat meat.
- Animal products contain large quantities of saturated fat, cholesterol, and have no dietary fiber. The U.S. Surgeon General has stated that 68% of all diseases are diet related. A diet rich in fruits, vegetables, and grains (and free from animal products) can prevent, improve, and sometimes cure breast cancer, osteoporosis, prostate cancer, impotence, and obesity.
- Seventy-five percent of federal poultry inspectors say they would not eat chicken.

Seeing the root cause of our problems is how we can begin to solve them most effectively. Each individual has the opportunity to make a difference in creating a sustainable world for ourselves and future generations. There is no escaping the ecological cost of eating meat, but there are ways to cut the price. One of the most significant choices you can make is to eat a vegetarian diet.

CHAPTER 1

Shop Smart— Cook Smarter

Having food in the kitchen is 90 percent of the cooking battle, so begin your vegetarian adventure with a trip to the supermarket. Check out natural food stores and ethnic groceries. Look for supermarkets and neighborhood co-ops that sell items from bins where you scoop out what you need. Without the excess packaging on the product, you save a lot of money and there is less to recycle. Farmers' markets are a great place to find cheap, often organically grown fresh fruits and vegetables. Avoid convenience stores, where prices are high.

Shop for produce and bread several times a week if you can. The old-fashioned advice to do a week's shopping in one trip falls apart when you choose to eat fresh vegetarian meals. It aims at people who buy canned fruit, frozen dinners, and preservative-laden bread. By buying fresh fruits and vegetables in small quantities, you won't find yourself staring at rotting produce in the refrigerator. If you shop more than once a week, you will find it easier to buy food that suits your mood.

The average supermarket carries over 20,000 items, and new products appear daily. Be aware that market researchers have found that when background music slows from 108 beats per minute to 60 beats per minute, supermarket sales increase by 40 percent. Enjoy the tunes, eat the free food samples, and shop with your own plan in mind.

As you roll your cart down the supermarket aisles, compare the price of the store labels with the same brand-name item. Store labels are usually cheaper and comparable or better in quality. Big food manufacturers pay supermarkets enormous slotting fees to gain shelf space, and brand name advertising budgets can reach over $100 million for a single product. As the consumer, you absorb the cost. Larger-sized packages are usually, but not always cheaper. Two 14-ounce cans of tomatoes may be cheaper than one 28-ounce can. Handwritten signs along the aisles often make shoppers think a product is on sale when it may not be. Get to know the price of the foods you buy so you will know a bargain when you see it.

Check the expiration dates on perishable foods like dairy products, cereals, and bread. The freshest product is usually in the back of the display, and a handwritten sign by a perishable item may be a way to get you to buy a product that is about to expire.

In the cereal aisle, the ready-to-eat, unsugared, whole grain cereals are usually on the bottom of the shelf, while the over-processed, sugar-laden cereals hit your eyes front and center. Read the labels and look for whole grain cereals like shredded wheat and Grape-Nuts. Unless you are still collecting the toy offers in the boxes, these cereals cost less and are better for you. Buying cereal grains like old-fashioned rolled oats and cooking them yourself will save you money, and they make hearty meals.

When you arrive at the checkout stand with a basket full of fresh vegetarian food, it may surprise you to find that your grocery bill is less than you expected. Dollar for dollar, you get a lot more grains, beans, fruits, and vegetables than meat.

A Guide for Picking and Keeping Some of the Best Stuff at the Market

The market can be an overwhelming place to a new vegetarian. How do you know you are getting the freshest produce? What does a parsnip look like? And where in the world is the tofu? Here is a guide that will help you overcome any anxiety you may have about selecting and storing soy foods and fresh, ripe fruits and vegetables.

Soy Foods

Just as whole kernels of wheat become flour for bread, pasta, and other foods, soybeans come in a variety of forms. Look for the following soy foods as you shop.

Miso A variety of misos are available ranging from hearty to light in taste. Miso is a thick puree made from the fermentation of soy beans, salt, and various grains. White or rice miso is mild and relatively sweet, red or barley miso is savory and versatile, and dark soy miso is thick and more strongly flavored. Miso adds rich flavor to soups, spreads, stews, and sauces. You will find it in natural food stores and Asian markets.

Soy Cheese Made from soy milk, soy cheese is similar but not identical to dairy cheese. Some soy cheese has casein added to make it melt when heated, and casein is a milk product. If you are a vegan looking to avoid all animal products, read the label on the cheese before tossing it into your shopping basket. You will find both hard and soft varieties of soy cheese. Gently aged tofu is whipped into a soft cheese with a creamy consistency, much like cream cheese. You will find firm soy cheese similar to mozzarella and Cheddar cheese.

Soy Milk This is a thick, dairy-free beverage made by blending soaked whole soybeans with water and straining out the pulp. You can use it in the same way you use cow's milk. Various brands taste surprisingly different from one another. If you don't like the first one you try, sample several others before you make a final decision about whether or not soy milk is for you. In cooked food, like soup for example, there is little taste difference between soy milk and cows' milk. Lightly sweetened, plain or vanilla soy milk is delicious poured on cereal, and it makes yummy chocolate pudding or "milk" shakes. Most soy milk is hermetically sealed to last months before opening; once opened, soy milk keeps for about 7 to 10 days in the refrigerator. Look for brands made from organic soybeans and fortified with calcium. You will find soy milk on a shelf, not in the dairy case.

Soy Yogurt Cultured from soy milk and available in many flavors, soy yogurt is lactose- and cholesterol-free. It has the texture of dairy yogurt, but it does not taste the same.

Soy Sauce The best soy sauce has no sugar, food coloring, or chemical additives. Both shoyu and tamari are Japanese-type soy sauces. Shoyu contains soybeans, wheat, water, and salt. Tamari is a by-product of miso-making and is saltier and more strongly flavored than shoyu, and it contains no wheat. It adds flavor and salt to soups, stews, sauces, and stir-fries. American, Japanese, and Chinese products are available in natural food stores, Asian groceries, and supermarkets.

Tempeh This cultured soybean product is a fermented soybean cake with a nutty aroma and chewy texture that may remind you of meat. Marinate it in soy sauce and then fry, grill, or steam it. Use it as a meat replacement in stir-fries or stews. Look for tempeh in most natural food stores either fresh or, more commonly, frozen. Thaw tempeh before using, but slice it while it's partially frozen to avoid crumbling.

Tofu   By itself, tofu has little taste, but the recipes in this book can help you turn tofu into one of your favorite fast foods. When tofu is produced, the process begins by separating the soy milk into curds and whey, and pressing the curds into blocks. You'll find four types of tofu available in American grocery stores.

Firm tofu is dense and solid and holds up well in stir-fries, soups, broiled, or on a grill—anywhere that you want it to maintain its shape.

Soft tofu is creamy and useful for dressing, dips, shakes, and desserts.

Silken tofu is made from a slightly different process. This results in a creamy, custard-like product. Silken tofu works well in pureed or blended dishes (*extra firm* silken tofu can be used in stir fries). In Japan, silken tofu is enjoyed as is with a touch of soy sauce and topped with chopped scallions.

Seasoned tofu is ready to eat straight from the package. It is a firm, dense tofu product produced by extracting the water under pressure, and cooking the solids with soy sauce and spices. Use it in sandwiches and savory dishes.

Tofu is usually found in the produce section of the supermarket, although some stores sell tofu in the dairy or deli sections. It is most commonly sold in water-filled tubs, vacuum packs, or aseptic packages. Check the expiration date on the package before you toss it into your shopping basket, and buy tofu as far ahead of the expiration date as possible.

Unless it is aseptically packaged, tofu should be kept cold. Once any tofu package is opened, left over tofu should be rinsed and covered with fresh water and stored in the refrigerator. To maintain freshness, change the water every other day. *Do not rinse and cover seasoned tofu with water.* If the tofu becomes slimy or sour, throw it away. Tofu can also be frozen up to five months. Defrosted tofu has a pleasant caramel color and a chewy, spongy texture that soaks up marinades and sauces and is great for the grill. Here's a chart to help you determine how best to keep your tofu fresh:

	BEFORE OPENING		AFTER OPENING	
	Store in Refrigerator	Store in Cupboard	Rinse and Cover with Fresh Water	Store in Refrigerator
Water-Filled Tubs	X		X	X
Vacuum Packs	X		X	X
Aseptic Packages	X	X	X	X
Seasoned Tofu	X			X

Fresh Produce

Try to buy fruits and vegetables where you can pick them individually instead of buying a packaged amount—that way you can avoid wilted and bruised produce. Even if they are a bargain, chances are you will end up discarding them. When you get home, remove fruit from plastic bags because plastic holds moisture and causes the fruit to mold. Unlike fruit, you should wrap most vegetables tightly in plastic. Store most fruits and vegetables in a cool place. They will usually keep the longest refrigerated. Store vegetables in their own crisper. If they are sitting with fruit, the ethylene gas from the fruit can cause premature brown spotting on vegetables. Do not wash fruits, particularly berries, before storing because it hastens their deterioration. Wash fruit immediately before serving.

Apples   If you find apples on sale, but the color is less than perfect, the quality of the fruit is probably still good inside. Avoid any that are soft or have bruised spots. Refrigerated apples will keep for two weeks or more.

Artichokes   Choose an artichoke that feels heavy for its size and has compact, fresh-looking leaves. Dark outer leaves sometimes indicate cold-weather damage. Don't let that stop you from buying it. Eating an artichoke is a unique experience. (See Artichoke Feast on page 182 for how to do it.)

Asparagus   Look for tightly closed, compact tips, and firm brittle stalks. Since they are hard to keep fresh, eat them as soon as possible.

Avocados   You know an avocado is ripe when it yields very slightly to the pressure of your thumb. If you must bring home one that's not quite ready for eating, you can hasten the ripening process by putting the avocado in a paper bag with a banana, at room temperature. Once ripe, avocados spoil quickly. A ready-to-eat avocado will keep in prime condition in the refrigerator for four to seven days.

Bananas   When buying bananas, buy some that are ripe, some not quite ripe, and a few green ones. That way they will be ready when you are. After a banana is ripe (but never before) you can put it in the refrigerator. Don't worry if the skin darkens after refrigeration. The fruit will still be good inside.

Beans   Green beans can be yellow or green depending on their variety. Their color should be bright, and they should snap easily and have a velvety feel. They will keep for about 5 days, refrigerated. Steam them until they are crisp-tender and eat them seasoned with salt and pepper and a splash of lemon juice.

Beets   Beet roots should be smooth and firm. They will keep for about 2 weeks in the refrigerator. Peel and then shred or grate raw beets and toss them into salads. If preparing cooked beets, trim the leaf stem to about one inch and boil or steam them with their skins on until tender. Lightly squeeze the beets when they are cool, and they will easily slip out of their jackets.

Broccoli   For the best flavor, choose broccoli with dark green florets and tiny buds. Yellowing florets and large thick stems are signs that broccoli is past its prime. Broccoli is delicious lightly steamed, sautéed, used in stir-fries, and eaten raw.

Brussels Sprouts   Look for small, firm, compact heads with bright green color. Avoid large puffy ones or heads with dark spots or insect damage. Overcooking results in mushy, bitter tasting vegetables. These minicabbages are tastiest when lightly steamed for 5 to 7 minutes. Cut off the stem end before steaming. Serve with a squeeze of lemon juice and season with salt and pepper.

Cabbage   Green and red cabbage have survived since pre-historic times. They are versatile, cheap, and will surprise you with how much flavor they add to vegetarian meals. Select a small, bright-colored, firm head that feels heavy for its size. Cabbage will keep for more than 2 weeks, refrigerated.

Cabbage, Chinese   This is a generic name for a variety of greens used in Asian cooking. Two of the most popular are bok choy and celery cabbage. Look for bok choy with dark green leaves and thick white stems. Cook the stems longer than the leaves. Celery cabbage should be uniformly light green. The entire vegetable is usable. Steam or sauté Chinese cabbages.

Cantaloupe   In selecting a cantaloupe be sure its exterior is covered with a creamy-colored netting. A large smooth spot is a bad sign, and the stem end should be smooth without rough fibers showing. Most important, it should have a sweet aroma. Wrap cut melons in plastic, and do not remove the seeds until you are ready to eat the melon since the seeds keep the melon moist.

Carrots   Look for carrots that are firm, not flabby. If the carrot is large and has a thick neck, the lighter-colored core will be large and thick, too. For eating purposes, the core should be small because the good taste comes from the deep orange outside that stores the sugar. Carrots do not need peeling.

Cauliflower   Buy compact white heads free of speckles and smudges. Eat it raw or cooked. It keeps for about a week refrigerated.

Chard, Swiss   This is really a beet grown for its leaves. If the stems are large and tough, discard them. If they are small, you can use them too. Before cooking, wash the leaves carefully to remove any sand that might cling to the leaves.

Collard Greens   Collard greens are cousins of cabbage and are available year-round. Look for bunches with crisp leaves and tender stems. Steam them with a sliver of garlic, and serve with a drizzle of olive oil.

Corn   Fresh sweet corn is a summer crop and is a vegetable that holds up well when frozen, so you can eat it year-round. If you buy frozen corn in bags, it is easy to scoop out just what you need.

Cucumbers When selecting cucumbers, make sure you know what *not* to buy. Over-mature cucumbers have a puffy, dull appearance. Eat cucumbers raw.

Eggplants Choose eggplants that are firm and have bright, shiny, dark skin. The cap should look fresh and green. Never eat eggplant raw—it contains a toxin called solanine. Cooking eliminates the danger. Once cooked, you can eat the skin if you desire. Eggplants submit to almost any cooking technique.

Garlic Look for good-sized garlic with plump cloves free of soft spots. It is easier and faster to peel one or two big cloves than six tiny ones. Unpeeled garlic will stay fresh for weeks. Store garlic in a cool, dry place, but not in the refrigerator. Refrigerate jars of garlic packed in oil.

Ginger Do not let these knobby looking roots scare you. Ginger is a fragrant addition to many vegetarian meals. Cover with plastic wrap and keep refrigerated for 2 weeks. You can also freeze ginger and grate it frozen. If the roots are large, you do not have to buy the whole thing; just break off an inch or two.

Grapefruit Choose grapefruits that are firm, spring to the touch, and feel heavy for their size. A heavy grapefruit indicates that it is full of juice. Grapefruit keeps for up to eight weeks, refrigerated.

Grapes Good grapes have a velvety, powdery appearance. Too much handling will give grapes a smooth and shiny look. If the stems look dry and brown, they are past their peak flavor.

Kale   This ruffled green is one of recorded history's oldest vegetables. The leaves feel tough and leathery, but once cooked, they become almost silky and soft. To keep kale and most other leafy greens crisp and fresh tasting, separate the leaves, rinse quickly, shake off the excess water, and enclose in a plastic bag in the refrigerator. Remove the leaves from the tough stems before cooking.

Kiwi   This fruit softens at room temperature and is ready to eat when it yields slightly to the touch. Scoop kiwis from the half shell, or peel and slice them into circles. They can be eaten like an apple, skin and all, although the skin is slightly tart. Store ripened kiwis in the refrigerator. They will last up to 3 weeks.

Leeks   Leeks are a member of the onion family, but less pungent in taste. Sand and dirt often collect in the leaves. You will find them in bunches of three or four, but you can buy just one.

Lemons and Limes   The best lemons and limes have a fine-textured skin and are heavy for their size. Avoid fruit that is soft or spongy feeling. Look at the stem; that's where signs of aging begin.

Lettuce   Lettuce is about the only produce that has managed to avoid becoming a processed food. You will not find it canned, frozen, or dehydrated. Forget iceberg lettuce, those tight round heads that look like green bowling balls. Pick leafy, dark green romaine or soft, loose-leafed Boston and Bibb lettuce instead.

Mushrooms   There are many varieties of mushrooms, but creminis or Italian mushrooms are the ones you are sure to see in most markets. Choose creminis with closed caps; when they open and look like umbrellas, it is a sign they have been hanging around the store too long. Store mushrooms in a paper bag in the refrigerator. They will keep for several days.

Onions There are many kinds of onions, but the most common, called white or yellow, are for cooking. Sweet onions, like Bermudas, are good in salads and sandwiches. Choose onions that have their protective skin, are symmetrical, and are heavy for their size. Avoid those with soft or discolored spots and "sprouters"; they are old. Store onions in a cool, dry place, and always keep a few on hand.

Oranges Do not depend on color to determine whether an orange is ripe and ready to eat. Instead, look for oranges that are firm and feel heavy for their size; this indicates lots of juice. Store them in the refrigerator for up to six weeks.

Parsnips Most people grow up without tasting parsnips. Try one if you are feeling adventurous. Parsnips look like an off-white carrot and have a unique nut-like flavor and a mild fragrance. Look for smooth, firm, well-shaped roots that are small to medium in size; large ones are likely to have woody cores. Peel them before using. They add sweetness to stews and soups and are tasty steamed, sautéed, or baked. They will keep for several weeks in the refrigerator.

Pears Growers pick pears before they are ripe, and they wind up in the produce department rock hard and bitter tasting. To achieve the sweet, buttery flavor that makes pears so delicious, ripen them in a warm place for two to three days or longer. Putting them in a perforated paper bag hastens the ripening process. They are ready to eat when the flesh around the stem yields to gentle pressure.

Peas, Garden and Chinese Snow Peas Most peas sold in markets are frozen. They are one of the few vegetables that hold their taste when processed. When you buy fresh peas, look for small, shiny green pods that are velvety to the touch. Don't buy pods that are filled to the bursting point. These are old or mature, and the peas inside will taste tough or mealy because the natural sugar has started to convert to starch. Also, reject any pods that are faded or discolored. Keep garden peas unshelled in the refrigerator and shell them just before using. Chinese snow peas are tiny inside and the pod is tender, so they are eaten whole. One of the best ways to enjoy fresh peas is to eat them raw. Use fresh peas as soon as possible.

Peppers, Bell Red, green, or yellow—they are all good. The green ones are usually the cheapest, and you can often use them interchangeably. However, for roasted red peppers, there is no substitution.

Potatoes Russet potatoes have a brown skin and are good for baking. White and red potatoes are good for all-around use: boiling, frying, mashing, and roasting. Watch out for potatoes with a greenish cast; they will taste bitter. Buy a few at a time if you are cooking for one person, and store them in a cool, dry place. It does not take long for a big bag of potatoes to start sprouting and grow moldy.

Spinach Look for prewashed spinach. It's ready to prepare. If you buy spinach by the bunch, float the leaves in a big pot or bowl of water. The sand that clings to the leaves will sink to the bottom.

Sprouts, Mung Bean Look for pearl-white sprouts that have not started to turn yellow. Store them for only 1 or 2 days in a sealed plastic bag in the refrigerator. Use them in stir-fries.

Squash, Summer Zucchini is the best known, and it's available year-round. Choose squash that are small for their size, crisp, and free of wrinkled skin. They will keep refrigerated for a week.

Squash, Winter Look for hard skin that shows no signs of softening or cracking. You will find winter squashes available in the supermarket year-round. Uncut squash will keep for months in a cool, dry place. Green and orange-colored winter squash can be a meal by themselves, used in soups, or stuffed with grains. Acorn and butternut are a good beginner's choice. They are "meaty" and flavorful and make a satisfying meal.

Tomatoes Look for tomatoes that are firm to the touch. Store ripe tomatoes in the refrigerator.

Turnips and Rutabagas These are close relatives, and they are interchangeable. Choose roots with firm, smooth skin and avoid very large ones, which may be woody and pithy. It is best to peel them before using because the skin can be chewy. Like carrots, they make good snacks eaten raw. They are delicious tossed into soups or stews, steamed, sautéed, and baked. They will keep refrigerated for 1 to 2 weeks.

Yams and Sweet Potatoes The items sold in American markets as "yams" are in fact a variety of sweet potato. (A true yam has a hairy, woody, brown exterior, and they are not widely available in the United States.) Do not substitute a true yam for a sweet potato. The pale yellow sweet potato you will find in most supermarkets has a pale yellow flesh and is dry and crumbly when cooked. The darker variety sweet potato, often mislabeled as a yam, has a dark orange flesh and is sweet and moist when cooked. Look for firm, plump, blemish-free potatoes. They'll keep for a few weeks stored in a cool, dry place. Do not refrigerate them unless they are already cooked. Sweet potatoes can be peeled and eaten raw for a snack or grated and eaten raw in salads. They lend themselves to baking, boiling, and roasting.

Shopping List

Keeping a well-stocked kitchen is as easy as buying an extra box of pasta or a can of beans when you are grocery shopping. Then if there is a blizzard, two days of nonstop exams, or you are sick and need to fend for yourself, you will have plenty to eat. Here is a handy list to help you shop.

Breads and Grains
- [ ] Brown rice
- [ ] Bulgur
- [ ] Cornmeal
- [ ] Couscous
- [ ] Oatmeal
- [ ] Pasta
- [ ] Rice noodles
- [ ] Tabbouleh
- [ ] Whole grain breads
- [ ] Whole grain ready-to-eat cereal

Canned Food
- [ ] Diced tomatoes
- [ ] Soup
- [ ] Spaghetti sauce
- [ ] Stewed tomatoes

Fresh Produce
- [ ] Apples
- [ ] Bananas
- [ ] Bell pepper
- [ ] Carrots
- [ ] Cilantro
- [ ] Garlic
- [ ] Gingerroot
- [ ] Jalapeño pepper
- [ ] Lemons
- [ ] Mushrooms
- [ ] Onions
- [ ] Oranges
- [ ] Potatoes
- [ ] Scallions
- [ ] Sprouts
- [ ] Sweet potatoes and yams
- [ ] Tomatoes

Nuts, Seeds, and Beans
- [ ] Beans: black, garbanzo, red kidney, white (canned or dried)

- ☐ Lentils
- ☐ Natural peanut butter
- ☐ Peas: black-eyed, split (canned or dried)
- ☐ Tahini
- ☐ Unsalted nuts

Condiments

- ☐ Canola oil
- ☐ Fruit spreads
- ☐ Hoisin sauce
- ☐ Maple syrup
- ☐ Olive oil
- ☐ Salsa
- ☐ Soy sauce
- ☐ Tabasco
- ☐ Vinegar

Refrigerated Items

- ☐ Cheeses
- ☐ Miso
- ☐ Soy milk or dairy milk
- ☐ Tofu
- ☐ Yogurt

Frozen Foods

- ☐ Corn
- ☐ Peas
- ☐ Pizza crust
- ☐ Tortillas

Beverages

- ☐ Coffee
- ☐ Fruit juice
- ☐ Tea, herbal
- ☐ Vegetable juice

CHAPTER 2

Tools, Techniques, and Terms

A Short Course

Most people learn how to cook through trial and error. Don't let cooking intimidate you. It's really very simple: You just apply heat over time, and things cook. There's much more latitude in cooking than you may think, and numbers are fairly arbitrary. If you like carrots, add more. If you don't like mushrooms, use less. As you become familiar with recipes, you won't feel the need to measure each 1/4 teaspoon of basil or 1/2 cup of chopped bell pepper. You will find many vegetarian recipes begin with cutting an onion, mincing a clove of garlic, or sautéing the vegetables for 3 to 5 minutes. This simple process can make the difference between food that is disappointing or simply delicious. With a little experience, cooking will become more creative and faster. Finally, it's just food, and it can't bite back.

People have managed for centuries to put elaborate meals on the table with little more than one pot, a skillet, a mixing bowl, a knife, a spoon, a spatula, and some source of heat. Fortunately, you can do it too. You don't need fancy equipment to prepare delicious vegetarian meals.

Tools You Will Need

Knives   Start with two sizes: a big knife (one that comfortably fits your hand), and one small paring knife for peeling and finer cuts. A good knife can be expensive, but it lasts a lifetime.

Pans   A medium-size 10-inch nonstick skillet is an ideal size. Many chefs stand by indestructible cast iron pans and stainless steel skillets. However, the new generation of nonstick cookware allows you to significantly cut down on the amount of oil you need for cooking. As a bonus, you will find clean up easier and faster.

Pots   A 3-quart or 4-quart capacity pot with a lid will work for most of your cooking. You may also need a larger pot if you're going to cook big batches of pasta or homemade chili. Get the best pots you can afford. Flimsy, thin-bottom cookware heats food unevenly and causes it to burn. Avoid aluminum pots because aluminum leaches into your food, upsetting your body's mineral balance.

Miscellaneous Tools   Here is a list of important items you will need:

baking dish
colander for draining cooked pasta
dish cloths, two
dish towels, two
handheld can opener—not electric (The Swing-A-Way
    brand is a good bet at about $4.)
handheld grater
measuring spoons (If you don't have measuring spoons, a
    regular teaspoon works fine. Remember that it takes
    three teaspoons to equal one tablespoon.)
mixing bowl

pot holders, two
potato masher
salad spinner
slotted long-handled spoon
slotted spatula
vegetable steamer basket or pot
wooden cutting board

Cutting Up Food

Knowing a few basic principles will help you cook efficiently and make food taste great. Good cooks soon attract hungry spectators, so look out—you may be serving your friends more often.

To reduce kitchen preparation time and to wield your knife like the cooks you see on TV, use a sharp knife. A knife is much more likely to slip and cut you if it is dull, and the food may turn out looking like it was run over by a bicycle tire.

For most cutting, hold the food in place with one hand, curling your fingers down to protect your fingertips. Hold the knife with your thumb and index finger gripping the top of the blade; this gives you good leverage.

Don't always cut things into tiny pieces. Cut larger pieces when possible to save time. Use large chunks for stews and smaller cuts for salads and stir-fries. Whenever appropriate, use unpeeled fruits and vegetables. To make cutting round food easy, first slice off a small portion to create a flat surface. Place the cut side down, and begin slicing pieces.

Know Your Terms

Chiffonade This is a way to cut large flat leaves like spinach and kale. Crumple and rumple the leaves into a ball, and hold them together with one hand while you cut with your other hand. Another method is to roll the leaves from end to end and slice into thin strips.

Chop   Cut foods into pieces about 1/2-inch square.

Dice or finely chop   Cut slices crosswise in each direction to create cubes or pieces ranging in size from 1/2 inch to 1/8 inch. To speed things up, bundle slices together and cut through the pile.

Grate   With a low-tech multisided grater, you can easily grate fresh vegetables and cheese for small salads and other meals. Grated foods add an interesting texture and lightness to dishes.

Mince   Garlic and gingerroot are commonly minced. Very small pieces tend to jump and scatter. Use the knife blade to push the pieces back into a heap to make cutting easier.

Slice   Make cuts about 1/2 inch apart for thick slices, 1/4 to 1/8 inch for thinner slices.

Cooking Terms

Baking and Roasting   What's the difference? There isn't any. Both terms describe preparing food with dry heat in an oven. Baking or roasting usually takes longer than most other cooking methods. Remember to preheat the oven so that it will be the right temperature when you are ready to begin cooking. This is especially important when baking cakes, breads, and cookies. Preheating also speeds up the cooking process.

Boiling and Simmering   Boiled foods cook in rapidly agitating liquid with bubbles breaking on the surface. Simmering involves more gently moving liquid, cooking just below the boiling point.

Braising   This is simmering foods in a small amount of liquid. Use vegetable stock, wine, soy sauce, or juices as all or part of the liquid to increase the flavor of the finished dish.

Add salt toward the end of cooking because salt concentrates as the liquids evaporate.

Broiling Broiling involves cooking in a preheated oven, with food approximately 3 to 4 inches from the heat. This method is fast and requires close attention because the heat is high and foods can quickly burn. Parboil (cook in rapidly boiling liquid) dense hard vegetables like potatoes or carrots for 5 minutes before broiling or grilling.

Microwaving Microwaves are good for reheating food and cooking a limited number of dishes. For truly wonderful tasting meals, use another cooking method. Never put metal items inside a microwave because they can cause dangerous sparking. If this happens, switch the oven off at once. Never turn the oven on when it is empty; microwaves may bounce off the walls and damage the cavity.

Sautéing Sautéing is a quick cooking method done on top of the stove. Food usually cooks in oil on medium or medium-high heat. Making sure the heat isn't too high can head off trouble. When you cook with a nonstick pan, you can use much less oil. When you heat the oil in the skillet before adding the food, the food will absorb less of it. To *sauté until soft* means to cook until the food is tender but not browned. To *sauté until brown* means to cook gently until the food is golden. A flavorful sauté is what gives real body to different dishes. It may seem like the liquid and starchy ingredients form the "base" or "soul" of pot foods like stews, soups, and beans. Actually they are more the "medium" that holds the bright flavors of your sauté.

Steaming Hot vapor produced by simmering or boiling water in a tightly covered pot cooks the food. Use a special two-piece steaming pot or stainless steel steaming basket inserted into a pot with a tight fitting lid. Keep the water level lower than the bottom of the steamer to avoid sogginess. Let the water come to a boil and then add the vegetables. Properly steamed vegetables are crisp and tender with good color.

Steaming times for vegetables will vary according to variety and cut sizes. Most vegetables cook in a matter of minutes. Brussels sprouts, cabbage, and cauliflower overcook quickly. You will know because your kitchen will start to stink. When preparing vegetables that require longer cooking, check the water level and add more water if it is boiling away. When you open the pot, tilt the lid so that the rising steam will move away from you.

Stir-Frying   Stir-frying is the Asian version of a hot, fast cooking technique. One of the advantages to this type of cooking is that you can cook a whole meal and use only one skillet or wok.

Chop and slice the vegetables and measure the seasoning before starting. Line up all of your ingredients near the stove. Heat a small amount of oil in a hot skillet then add the garlic, the seasonings for flavoring the whole dish, and vegetables a handful at a time. When you cook with garlic, don't add it by itself. It will burn. Avoid overcrowding the pan, otherwise, you'll end up with soggy food. Begin by tossing in the hard vegetables first and progress to softer vegetables. Always keep the food in motion—stir and fry. The last things you add are liquid seasonings like soy sauce. Remove the vegetables from the pan quickly to maintain crispness.

Never immerse a hot pan in cold water—this can warp the metal. Let the pan cool slightly, then add water.

Food Preparation Techniques

Asparagus   Snap off their tough, white bottoms and hold them under gently running water to remove any sand. Cook them in boiling water or steam them just until their color brightens and they are tender. Serve with a splash of olive oil and lemon juice.

Avocado   Slice the avocado in half lengthwise. Remove the seed. Cut lengthwise and crosswise slices in the flesh making a grid. Scoop the avocado cubes out of the shells with a spoon.

Beets   Wash beets and steam or boil them until tender. Peel beets after they're cooked; the skins will slip off easily.

Chiles   The heat from chiles is in the ribs and seeds that are inside. Cut the chile open like a book, and remove ribs and seeds. Avoid touching your eyes or face while handling chiles.

Cucumber   Peel the wax-coated skin before eating cucumbers.

Garlic   First remove a clove from the bulb. Peel the clove by putting it on a cutting board and gently smashing it with the side of a large knife. The skin will slip off and the flattened garlic is easy to use. If you need small pieces, chop or mince by rocking your knife blade across the garlic. Hold down the front of the knife with the palm of your hand, and cut, repeatedly pushing the garlic pieces back into a heap as you go.

Gingerroot   Thin-skinned gingerroot needs no peeling. The strongest flavor is just beneath the skin.

Greens   To prepare kale, chard, collards, or turnip greens, first discard any yellow or damaged leaves. Strip the leaves from large or tough stems and discard the stems. To cut the leaves, stack, bundle, or crumple them together with one hand while you slice with the other hand.

Leeks   Sand and dirt often collect in the leaves. Slice them in half lengthwise, separate the layers, and rinse them with cool water, gently rubbing away the grit.

Lemons   Get more juice from lemons by gently rolling them on the counter and applying pressure with your hand before you cut them. This helps break the interior cells of the fruit. If you don't have a lemon squeezer, insert a fork into the center of a cut lemon and twist to juice.

Mushrooms   Just before using fresh mushrooms, wipe them with a paper towel. Do not wash them, or they'll become water logged and have less flavor when cooked.

Onions   Cut off the root and stem ends, slice in half lengthwise, peel off the skin and outer layer of the onion, and chop. If you only need 1/2 an onion, chop the whole thing, and store what's left in the refrigerator. It will keep several days, and you'll have a head start on tomorrow's meal. If chopping an onion causes your eyes to water, chilling the onion in the refrigerator for a few minutes will help ease the problem. Onions contain a substance called sulphur oxide. When it comes in contact with the moisture in your eyes, it forms a compound similar to sulfuric acid. That's why your eyes burn.

Potatoes   Pare off potato eyes, green spots, and blemishes. Otherwise, don't bother to peel potatoes.

Squash, Winter   Don't peel a squash before baking it. Simply cut in half and cook it cut-side down. Raw squash added to soups and stews will require peeling.

Sweet Potatoes   Don't peel whole sweet potatoes or yams before baking, but do peel them for stews and soups.

Tofu   Depending on the dish you're making, you may want to make tofu firmer by pressing out some of the water. Strange as the pressing process may sound, give it a try. Pressed tofu grills beautifully. If you want cubes of tofu to become brown and crispy in a stir-fry and to hold their shape, pressing works wonders. Sandwich the tofu between two plates. Weight the top plate with a heavy book for 30 minutes. Sometimes the top plate slides off the tofu during the pressing process. Keep the plates away from the edge of a counter or table. After about 30 minutes, remove the weight and top plate, and drain the water from the bottom plate. The tofu is now ready to slice and use.

Tomatoes   Don't bother to peel them.

Turnips   Older roots can have tough skins, so peel them.

Season to Taste

Research in the fields of chemistry and psychology suggests that specific aromas can increase brain power and the ability to concentrate. A study at the University of Cincinnati demonstrated that people in a room scented with peppermint had more correct answers to test questions than people taking the same test in unscented rooms. So take a deep breath when you are seasoning food in the kitchen. As you experiment, you'll learn how some seasonings and foods naturally go together. The more you use seasonings, the more your seasoning sense will become second nature.

Herbs and Spices

For starters, begin with a few basic dried herbs and spices: basil, cinnamon, cumin, curry, dill, mint, oregano, thyme, and rosemary.

It is best to buy herbs and spices in the smallest possible amounts, and store them in tightly closed bottles in a cool, dry spot out of direct light. Replace seasonings after six months to a year when their aroma and taste have faded. When substituting dried herbs for fresh ones, use about one-third the amount called for in the recipe. Cilantro and parsley are two herbs that must be fresh. Dried parsley tastes like straw, and dried cilantro doesn't resemble the fresh version at all. Most people love fresh cilantro, but taste it before you toss a handful into something you're cooking. Substitute parsley if you don't like the taste.

Sophisticated Tastes

Condiments from around the globe, once found only in expensive gourmet grocery stores, are now on the shelves of well-stocked supermarkets. Just open a bottle or jar and add instant, striking flavor to your meals. Chutney can jazz up plain baked potatoes, winter squash, and bagels. If you like your food "hot 'n' spicy," Szechwan sauce and Vietnamese red chili sauce can perk up main dish meals. Hoisin sauce, often called the catsup of Asia, is a popular table condiment for a variety of dishes including stir-fries. It is made from soy sauce, garlic, and chile with the sweet flavor of anise. Hoisin sauce is a great marinade for tofu. A splash of special vinegar can give oven-roasted potatoes, cooked vegetables, soup, and even a pot of beans a wonderful boost. Tahini made from ground sesame seeds adds interesting flavor to many dishes and dips. Buy a jar or can and keep it on hand in the refrigerator. Hot pepper sesame oil gives stir-fries real character. It costs about $4, but its powerful flavor makes a small bottle last a long time. Don't forget the ever popular salsa, Tabasco, catsup, and mustard for flavoring food.

CHAPTER 3

Breakfast Anytime

On most mornings, cold cereal and a bagel will do, but if you are ready for more, you will find quick eating ideas in this chapter. There is a recipe for oatmeal that "cooks" by itself while you sleep. Or try scrambled tofu instead of the usual eggs. This weekend, surprise your friends with a beer pancake brunch. After a long fast from a night of sleep, breakfast seems like a praiseworthy idea, and if breakfast begins at noon because of the late hours you keep, you will find breakfast ideas in this chapter that are delicious any time of the day.

French Toast 2000

PREPARATION TIME: 5 minutes
COOKING TIME: 12 minutes

If you're looking for a quick breakfast, soak the bread in the batter the night before, cover, and refrigerate until morning. They take just a few minutes to cook.

1/2	cup soy milk or dairy milk
2	egg whites
1/4	teaspoon vanilla
1/4	teaspoon ground cinnamon
1	teaspoon sugar (optional)
4	slices multigrain bread
1/2	to 1 teaspoon vegetable oil

1. In a shallow pan or bowl, whisk together the milk, egg whites, vanilla, cinnamon, and sugar.

2. Dip the slices of bread into the milk mixture one by one, turning to coat both sides.

3. Heat a lightly oiled, medium nonstick skillet on medium heat and fry the bread until it is lightly browned on both sides. Serve topped with maple syrup, sliced fruit, applesauce, or your favorite fruit spread.

NOTE: This recipe may be made without egg whites if you wish.

Yield: 2 servings

Fluffy Vegan Pancakes

PREPARATION TIME: 4 minutes
COOKING TIME: 3 to 4 minutes per pancake

This eggless recipe makes light and fluffy pancakes by whipping the liquid ingredients with a fork for 1 minute until frothy.

1	cup whole wheat flour
1	cup unbleached white flour
1	tablespoon baking powder
2	cups soy milk
1	tablespoon vegetable oil

1. Stir the flours and baking powder together in a large bowl. In a separate bowl, combine the soy milk and oil, and whip for about 1 minute. Pour the soy mixture into the flour mixture. Stir just to combine. Don't worry about lumps.

2. Lightly oil a medium nonstick skillet. Heat over medium heat. When a few drops of water sprinkled on the skillet sizzle or bead up, the pan is ready.

3. Pour 1/4 cup of the batter at a time onto the skillet. Cook until the pancakes begin to bubble, about 3 minutes. Turn with a spatula, and cook until the second side is lightly browned. Serve with maple syrup.

Yield: About 8 (4-inch) pancakes

NOTE: If you like thin pancakes, add more soy milk a tablespoon at a time.

Beer Pancakes

PREPARATION TIME: 5 minutes
COOKING TIME: About 3 minutes for each pancake

Eat these intriguing pancakes for breakfast or dessert. They are a good way to use up leftover beer from a party.

1³/4 cups whole wheat flour
1¹/2 teaspoons baking powder
¹/2   teaspoon baking soda
1   egg
3   tablespoons oil
1   tablespoon honey
1   can or bottle (12 ounces) beer

1. In a large bowl, combine the flour, baking powder, and baking soda, and mix well. In another bowl, whisk together the egg, oil, and honey with a fork.

2. Add the liquid mixture and the beer to the dry ingredients; stir just until a smooth batter is formed. The batter will be somewhat lumpy and slightly thick.

3. Lightly oil a medium nonstick skillet, and place it over medium heat until hot. Pour ¹/4 cup of the batter at a time onto the skillet. Cook the pancakes until the bottoms are golden brown and the tops begin to bubble. Flip them over, and cook until the undersides are golden brown. Serve with maple syrup.

Yield: About 14 (4-inch) pancakes

Banana French Toast

PREPARATION TIME: 6 minutes
COOKING TIME: 8 to 12 minutes

This recipe is made without eggs and produces a moist, delicious meal. You'll need a nonstick skillet to keep the natural sugar that is in the banana and the juice from sticking to the pan. You'll also need a blender to mix the batter.

1	cup sliced ripe banana
3/4	cup soy milk or orange juice
1/2	teaspoon ground cinnamon
4	to 5 slices whole wheat bread
1/2	to 1 teaspoon vegetable oil

1. Combine the banana, soy milk or orange juice, and cinnamon in a blender; blend until smooth. Pour the mixture into a shallow pan or bowl.

2. Dip the bread into the batter and turn it gently to coat both sides.

3. Lightly oil a nonstick skillet and heat over medium heat until hot Add the coated bread slices, and fry them until they are golden brown, 2 to 3 minutes on each side. Serve with maple syrup.

Yield: 1 to 2 servings

Hot Oats and Raisins

PREPARATION TIME: 5 minutes
COOKING TIME: 8 minutes

This thick, creamy oatmeal is a tasty recipe to add to your regular repertoire. It is good any time of the day.

1	cup soy milk or dairy milk
1/2	cup rolled oats (regular or quick, not instant)
2	tablespoons raisins
1/2	apple, peeled and chopped
1	tablespoon chopped walnuts
1/4	teaspoon ground cinnamon
1/2	teaspoon sugar (optional)

1. In a saucepan, combine the milk, oats, raisins, and apple. Bring to a boil; reduce the heat, cover the pan, and simmer the cereal, stirring it often, for about 4 minutes.

2. Turn off the heat, and let the pot rest for another minute or two, or until the oatmeal reaches the desired consistency.

3. Serve sprinkled with the nuts, cinnamon, and sugar if you wish. Add a splash of milk if you desire.

Yield: 1 serving

Overnight Oatmeal

PREPARATION TIME: 4 minutes

Too busy to cook breakfast? Wake up to breakfast ready and waiting.

1   cup old-fashioned rolled oats
1   cup soy milk or dairy milk
1   tablespoon raisins
1/2 teaspoon ground cinnamon
1   cup diced seasonal fruit (optional)

1. In a cereal bowl, combine the oats, milk, raisins, and cinnamon. Cover and refrigerate overnight.
2. In the morning stir in fresh fruit if you desire, and breakfast is ready. Serve it chilled.

Yield: 1 to 2 servings

Scrambled Tofu Curry

PREPARATION TIME: 7 minutes

Try scrambled tofu for breakfast; if that doesn't work, try pancakes. They don't resemble tofu at all.

5	ounces firm or extra-firm tofu (packaged in tubs of water)
1/2	teaspoon oil
1	tablespoon finely sliced scallion (about 1/2)
1	tablespoon diced green or red bell pepper (about 1/8)
2	tablespoons diced carrot (about 1/4 medium)
1/4	teaspoon curry powder
	Salt and pepper

1. In a shallow bowl or plate, lightly mash the tofu with a fork so that it resembles the texture of scrambled eggs. Set it aside.

2. Heat the oil in a small skillet over medium heat. Sauté the scallion, pepper, carrot, and curry for 2 to 3 minutes, or until the vegetables begin to soften. Reduce the heat to low, and stir in the tofu; cook for about 1 minute or until the mixture is hot. Serve immediately. Salt and pepper to taste.

Yield: 1 serving

Greek-Style Scrambled Tofu

PREPARATION TIME: 7 minutes

5   ounces firm or extra-firm tofu
1/2   teaspoon olive oil
1/4   cup chopped scallion (include green end, 1 large or
      2 small)
2   cloves garlic, minced
1/4   teaspoon dried oregano
1   cup tightly packed chopped fresh spinach
2   to 3 tablespoons crumbled feta cheese

1. In a shallow bowl or plate, lightly mash the tofu with a fork
   so that it resembles the texture of scrambled eggs. Set it
   aside.

2. Heat the oil in a medium nonstick skillet over medium heat.
   Sauté the scallion, garlic, and oregano for 30 seconds, and
   add the spinach. Cook, stirring until the spinach wilts,
   about 3 minutes. The water that remains on the spinach
   from washing will be enough to cook the spinach.

3. Reduce the heat to low. Add the tofu and gently stir until the
   mixture is warm, about 1 minute. Stir in the feta cheese,
   and serve immediately. Season with salt and pepper if you
   desire.

Yield: 1 serving

Polenta Hot Cakes

PREPARATION TIME: 3 minutes
COOKING TIME: About 5 minutes

Here is a delicious way to use leftover polenta.

Slices of cooked, cooled polenta
Vegetable oil
Maple syrup
Fresh fruit (optional)

1. Cut the polenta into 1/2-inch slices. Lightly oil a nonstick skillet with vegetable oil, and set it over medium-high heat until hot. Add the polenta and fry until it is warm and slightly crispy.
2. Serve with maple syrup. Add slices of fresh fruit if you desire.

Yield: 1 serving

Rice Pudding Cereal

PREPARATION TIME: 6 minutes
COOKING TIME: About 60 minutes

Eat this pudding for dessert or breakfast. It is easy to prepare if you have leftover rice, and it's good enough to justify cooking rice especially for it.

2	cups cooked brown rice
1/2	cup raisins
1	teaspoon ground cinnamon
2	cups soy milk or dairy milk
2	tablespoons sugar
1	teaspoon vanilla
1/4	teaspoon nutmeg (optional)
1	pear or apple, peeled, cored, and finely chopped (optional)

Preheat the oven to 325 degrees F.

1. In a 6-cup baking dish, mix together rice, raisins, and cinnamon. Add milk, sugar, and vanilla. Gently stir. Add the nutmeg and pear or apple if you desire.

2. Bake the pudding for 15 minutes and stir. Bake for another 45 to 50 minutes, until the milk is nearly absorbed.

3. Remove the dish from the oven. As the pudding cools, the rice will absorb any liquid that remains. Serve the pudding warm or chilled.

Yield: 4 servings

Tomato Shake

PREPARATION TIME: 3 minutes

If you like gazpacho, you will love this creamy tomato drink. You need a blender for this recipe.

1/4	cup plain yogurt
1	cup tomato juice
1	clove garlic, chopped
1/4	cup peeled, chopped cucumber
1	teaspoon seeded, chopped jalapeño pepper
	Dash of hot pepper sauce (optional)

Combine the ingredients in a blender. Add a dash of hot pepper sauce if you desire.

Yield: 1 serving

Tofu Berry Shake

This is an amazingly luxurious shake. You will never recognize tofu in this form. Honest, this is sooooo delicious.

1   (6 ounce) can pineapple juice
1   ripe banana
1/2 cup silken tofu (4 ounces)
1/2 to 1 cup fresh or frozen strawberries
1/2 teaspoon vanilla
1   to 2 tablespoons sugar (optional)

Combine all ingredients except the sugar in a blender and puree until smooth. Taste. Add sugar if you desire.

Yield: 2 servings

Yogurt Fruit Shake

PREPARATION TIME: **4 minutes**

Got a blender? Here's a fast way to start the day.

3/4   cup plain nonfat yogurt
1   cup chopped fruit (pear, pineapple, banana—the riper
        the better)
1/2   teaspoon vanilla
1   teaspoon honey or sugar (optional)

Place ingredients in blender, and process until smooth.

Yield: 1 to 2 servings

CHAPTER 4

Dips and Spreads

The recipes in this chapter are premium formulas for fast food. Combine these dips and spreads with crusty bread, crackers, chips, and vegetables and voilà you have the makings for simple meals or great snacks. Whip up a bowl of hummus and have a feast! What could be more heavenly than guacamole scooped onto tortillas or toast? If you're in a hurry, take a moment to make one of the recipes in this chapter—it's worth it!

Fresh Salsa

PREPARATION TIME: 6 minutes

You'll find salsa on the shelves of every supermarket, but for a real treat, make your own. For the kick in your salsa, cilantro is a must. Most of the heat in chiles comes from the seeds inside. If you want to lower the fire, cut the pepper lengthwise, and remove the seeds and veins.

3	cups chopped tomatoes (3 medium)
1/2	cup chopped cilantro
1/4	cup chopped green onion (3 or 4 medium)
1	tablespoon minced jalapeño pepper (about 1 medium)
3	tablespoons fresh lemon or lime juice (about 1 medium)
1	clove garlic, minced
	Salt

In a medium bowl, mix all ingredients together.

Yield: About 3 cups

Tsiziki Sauce and Dip

PREPARATION TIME: 6 minutes

Dip fresh vegetables and chunks of French bread into this garlicky sauce. Use it as a dressing for green salads, grain dishes, and pocket bread sandwiches. Adjust the number of garlic cloves to suit your taste. Tsiziki keeps well in the refrigerator for 3 to 4 days.

1	large cucumber, peeled and finely chopped
1	cup plain nonfat yogurt
1	teaspoon dried dill weed
4	large cloves garlic, minced
1	tablespoon fresh lemon juice
	Salt

Combine all the ingredients in a bowl. If you can wait, let it stand at room temperature for 20 minutes. Dive in. Store leftover sauce in the refrigerator. It will keep for 3 to 4 days.

Yield: 1 1/2 cups

Tahini Dipping Sauce

PREPARATION TIME: 5 minutes

This sauce turns a platter of steamed vegetables into a feast. It is good spooned over baked sweet potatoes and grain dishes. It will keep in the refrigerator for a week or longer.

1	cup nonfat yogurt
2	teaspoons tahini
1	clove garlic, minced
1 1/2	teaspoons lemon juice
1/8	teaspoon salt
	Pepper

Whisk together all of the ingredients and store it in the refrigerator.

Yield: 1 cup

Guacamole –
The Real Thing

PREPARATION TIME: 5 minutes

Here is a recipe for transforming an ordinary fruit into one of the world's greatest dips. If you can use a fork, you can make guacamole ("avocado sauce" in Spanish). Use it as a dip with chips or as a topping for burritos, tacos, and quesadillas.

1	avocado (slightly overripe works best)
1	tablespoon fresh lemon or lime juice (to prevent browning)
	Tabasco sauce
1/8	teaspoon salt (optional)

1. Slice the avocado in half lengthwise, and gently twist to remove the seed. Make lengthwise and crosswise cuts into the flesh every 1/2 inch. Scoop the avocado cubes into a bowl. Mash the avocado with a fork.

2. Add the extras: fresh lemon or lime juice, Tabasco, and salt if you desire.

Yield: About 1 cup

Roasted Garlic

PREPARATION TIME: 4 minutes
COOKING TIME: About 60 minutes

This wonderful spread or topping is delicious on crusty French bread, baked potatoes, and pizza. Use it to replace mayonnaise on sandwiches. Once cooked, garlic's strong smell disappears, and the flavor becomes sweet and buttery. To eat it, gently squeeze the large end of the cooked clove, and the garlic will slip out of the shell.

3   heads of garlic

Preheat the oven to 350 degrees F.

1. Carefully remove the outer papery skin from the garlic heads. Leave the heads intact and do not break them apart into cloves.

2. Carefully cut the top 1/2 inch off of each head. Arrange the garlic heads in a small baking dish so they fit comfortably.

3. Add enough water to cover the bottom of the dish with 1/4 inch of water. Cover with a lid or seal the dish with foil and bake for about 60 minutes until the cloves are soft to the touch. Roasted garlic will last for at least a week in a covered container in the refrigerator.

Yield: About 1/3 cup

Eggplant and Garlic Spread

PREPARATION TIME: 10 minutes

Sumptuous eggplant dip can be a meal when surrounded with toasted pita bread and fresh vegetables. Broiling an eggplant is as simple as deflating a balloon. It is done cooking when the eggplant is completely wrinkled, limp, and soft.

1	eggplant (about 1 pound)
2	tablespoons tahini
2	tablespoons fresh lemon juice
1	large clove garlic, finely minced
2	tablespoons minced onion
	Salt and pepper
1	teaspoon olive oil (optional)
1	tablespoon minced fresh parsley (optional)

Preheat the broiler.

1. Prick the eggplant in several places with a fork, and cut off the stem end. Place the eggplant on a baking sheet, and broil for 20 minutes or until done, turning the vegetable several times so that the skin chars on all sides.

2. When the eggplant is cool enough to handle, cut it in half; scrape out the flesh into a bowl. Discard the skin, and mash the eggplant with a potato masher or fork. Add the tahini, lemon juice, garlic, onion, and salt and pepper to taste.

3. If you have time, cover the spread and refrigerate it for a few hours. Before serving, sprinkle it with oil and parsley if you desire.

Yield: About 1 1/2 cups

Hummus

Hummus is a rich pâté made from garbanzo beans. If you've never eaten hummus, you're in for a classic treat. Keep a bowl of hummus on hand, and use it to make a superior sandwich piled high with greens, tomatoes, and sprouts. Hummus will keep for several days in a covered container in the refrigerator. You can create an entire meal around a plateful of hummus with toasted bread or warm pocket bread for dipping and a salad.

1	(15-ounce) can garbanzo beans, drained (about 1¹/₂ cups)
6	to 7 tablespoons fresh lemon juice (1 large or 2 small)
2	cloves garlic, minced
2	to 3 tablespoons tahini
2	tablespoons minced onion
2	tablespoons minced fresh parsley (optional)
	Salt

1. Mash the garbanzo beans into a thick paste using a masher, fork, or blender. Add the lemon juice, garlic, tahini, onions, and parsley if you wish; stir.

2. Hummus should have a consistency similar to mayonnaise. If it seems too thick, add more lemon juice, 1 tablespoon at a time. Taste; season with salt if you desire.

Yield: About 1³/₄ cups

CHAPTER 5

Soups and Stews

Forget the idea that homemade soup takes hours to prepare. Although opening a can of soup is convenient, the soups you will find here are surprisingly quick to make. Miso-Happy Soup is good for breakfast and dinner. You will find a recipe for Impulse Minestrone, and if you like creamy soup, you'll enjoy Corn and Potato Chowder.

"A good soup gathers chairs," so invite your friends, and have a party.

Miso-Happy Soup

<small>PREPARATION TIME:</small> 3 minutes
<small>COOKING TIME:</small> 3 to 5 minutes

Miso is a concentrated, fermented pâté made from soybeans and has the consistency of creamy peanut butter. It makes a delicate clear soup in minutes. A cup of miso soup can be a satisfying one-bowl pick-me-up when you want something warm to take the chill out of a night of studying, or it can be a quick breakfast. In Japan it's part of the traditional Japanese morning meal along with rice.

You will find miso in Japanese and Chinese markets, natural food stores, and some supermarkets. It keeps almost indefinitely in the refrigerator. Miso comes in many flavors. For starters try red miso, barley miso, or Hatcho miso.

Sip a modest cup of miso soup, or try an extravagant version with tofu and onions. The variations on this soup are endless. Just remember, for best results use vegetables in small amounts and cook them only slightly.

2	cups water
4	onion slices, cut into very thin half moons
1/4	cup carrots, cut into thin matchsticks
1/4	cup tofu, cut into small cubes
1	tablespoon miso
	Dash of pepper
1	tablespoon chopped scallion (optional)

1. Combine the water, onion, and carrots in a small covered saucepan and simmer for 3 to 5 minutes. Add the tofu.

2. Place the miso in a cup with about 1/4 cup cooking broth. Mix until all the miso is dissolved; add it to the soup. Do not boil after the miso is added. (High heat destroys miso's beneficial enzymes.) Season with pepper and garnish with scallions if you desire.

Yield: 2 servings

Impulse Minestrone Soup

PREPARATION TIME: 6 minutes
COOKING TIME: 10 minutes

This soup always turns out wonderfully, and it never needs to be the same. Start with one can each of stewed tomatoes and canned beans and add from there. If you are using frozen vegetables, buy them in bags rather than boxes. It's easier to scoop out the amount you need.

1	teaspoon olive oil
1	large clove garlic, finely chopped
1	cup chopped zucchini (about $1/2$ medium)
$1/2$	teaspoon dried basil
$1/8$	teaspoon dried oregano
1	cup frozen mixed vegetables
1	cup canned kidney beans, drained
1	($14^{1/2}$-ounce) can diced tomatoes
1	cup water
2	cups uncooked spiral pasta
	Salt and pepper
	Grated Parmesan (optional)

1. Heat the oil in a medium saucepan on medium heat. Sauté the garlic, zucchini, basil, and oregano, and cook, stirring, for 2 to 3 minutes. Add the mixed vegetables, beans, tomatoes, and water. Simmer for 10 minutes.

2. While the soup warms, cook the pasta in a small saucepan of boiling water for 7 to 9 minutes. Drain. Add the pasta to the soup.

3. Remove the soup from the heat and serve. Season with salt and pepper to taste. Sprinkle with grated Parmesan if you desire.

Yield: 2 servings

Split Pea Soup

PREPARATION TIME: 18 minutes
COOKING TIME: About 40 minutes

Here chipotle peppers are used to add a hot, smoky flavor to the soup. You'll find chipotle peppers in cans packed in adobo sauce in the Mexican section of the supermarket. Wash your hands after cutting chiles because they can cause a burning sensation on your skin. Store leftover chiles in a container in the freezer.

2	teaspoons olive oil
1	cup chopped onion (1 small)
2	large cloves garlic, minced
2	medium carrots, chopped (about 2 cups)
4	cups water
1	cup dried, green split peas
2	chipotle peppers, chopped (optional)
2	cups cubed potatoes (about 2 medium)
1/4	teaspoon salt

1. Heat the oil in a 3- to 4-quart saucepan; sauté the onion and garlic on medium heat until the onion is tender, about 5 minutes, stirring occasionally. Add the carrots and continue cooking and stirring occasionally for another 3 to 5 minutes. Add the water, peas, and chipotles (if desired).

2. Cover the pot and bring it to a boil. Reduce the heat to low and simmer, covered, until the peas are tender (about 30 minutes) stirring occasionally.

3. When the peas are tender, cut the potatoes in half lengthwise and then cut them into $1/4$-inch slices. Add the potatoes to the pot and cook until they are tender, about 15 minutes. Add the salt. Serve with slices of crusty multigrain bread.

NOTE: You can prepare the soup without the chipotle peppers, and it's still delicious—simply season to taste with salt and pepper.

Yield: 4 servings

Barley Mushroom Soup

PREPARATION TIME: 20 minutes
COOKING TIME: About 45 minutes

This recipe turns water, barley, and a few vegetables into a satisfying, thick soup. It is amazing what a slow, 10-minute sauté can do to flavor the simplest ingredients. A pound of barley costs about $.35 and can make four big pots of soup.

1	tablespoon chopped dried shiitaki mushrooms (about 2)
1/2	cup hot water for soaking mushrooms
1	tablespoon olive oil
1	cup chopped onion (about 1 small)
1	cup sliced fresh mushrooms (3 to 4)
1	cup thinly sliced carrot (about 1)
1/2	cup chopped celery (1 stalk)
1/2	cup pearl barley
2	tablespoons flour
3	cups water
1/2	teaspoon salt
	Pepper

1. Soften the shiitaki mushrooms in hot water for 10 minutes, and then dice the mushrooms. Reserve the soaking liquid. Heat the oil in a 3- or 4-quart pot over medium heat. Add the shiitake mushrooms, onions, fresh mushrooms, carrot, celery, and barley. Sauté on medium-low heat for about 10 minutes, stirring frequently so the vegetables and barley do not burn. Keep an eye on the bottom of the pot and reduce the heat if the sauté is sticking or browning too quickly.

2 Add the flour, stirring continually for 1 minute. Immediately add 3 cups of water and the mushroom soaking liquid. Scrape the bottom of the pot with a big spoon to incorporate any flour that may stick to the bottom. This step is important because the flavor from the sauté is in the stuff that may be on the bottom of the pot. Continue scraping and stirring until the bottom of the pot feels smooth, about 1 minute.

3. Add the salt. Bring to a boil, then reduce the heat. Cover and simmer for about 45 minutes or until the barley is tender. Stir the pot occasionally as the soup cooks. Taste for seasoning, and add salt and pepper if necessary.

Yield: 2 to 3 servings

Corn and Potato Chowder

PREPARATION TIME: 10 minutes
COOKING TIME: About 20 minutes

This easy-to-prepare chowder has the richness of a creamed soup without the cream.

1	tablespoon olive oil
1	cup chopped onion (about 1 small)
1	cup thinly sliced celery (2 medium stalks)
4	cups peeled russet potatoes, cut into 1/2-inch cubes (2 to 3 medium)
3¼	cups soy milk or lowfat dairy milk
1	cup frozen corn kernels, thawed
1/2	cup frozen peas, thawed (optional)
1/4	teaspoon salt
	Pepper
	Minced fresh parsley (optional)

1. Heat the oil in a 3- to 4-quart saucepan. Add the onion and celery and sauté over medium heat until the vegetables soften, 7 to 8 minutes, stirring frequently.

2. Add the potatoes and milk. Cover and simmer until the potatoes are tender, about 20 minutes. Mash some of the potatoes in the pot with a potato masher to thicken the soup. Add the corn kernels. If you like peas, add them too. Cook just until heated through, 1 to 2 minutes. Add the salt, and season with pepper to taste.

3. Ladle the soup into a bowl, and sprinkle with parsley if you desire.

Yield: 3 servings

Tomato Soup

PREPARATION TIME: 6 minutes
COOKING TIME: 45 minutes

Buy a loaf of crusty hearth bread to accompany the soup, and you've got a great meal.

1	teaspoon olive oil
1	cup finely chopped onion (about 1/2 medium)
2	cloves garlic, finely chopped
1/2	teaspoon dried dill
2	(14 1/2-ounce) cans chopped tomatoes, undrained
1	medium fresh tomato, chopped
1 1/2	teaspoons honey
1/2	cup water
	Salt and pepper
	Plain nonfat yogurt (optional)
1	tablespoon chopped fresh parsley (optional)

1. Heat the oil in a 3- or 4-quart pot over medium heat. Add the onion and garlic and sauté 5 to 8 minutes until the onion is soft, stirring frequently. Add the dill, canned tomatoes, fresh tomato, honey, and water. Stir.

2. Cover and simmer 45 minutes on low heat. Remove from the heat. Season to taste with salt and pepper.

3. Ladle the soup into a bowl. Top with a big dollop of yogurt and sprinkle with parsley if you desire.

Yield: 2 to 3 servings

Lentil Soup

PREPARATION TIME: 15 minutes
COOKING TIME: 50 minutes

Use the chop-and-toss method to make this delicious soup. While the lentils cook, cut up the vegetables. Pitch them into the pot and simmer until tender. What could be easier? Even though this recipe has a long list of ingredients, there are several vegetables that can be left out, and you'll still wind up with a delicious pot of soup.

1/2	cup lentils
2 1/2	cups water
1	medium carrot, chopped
2	green onions with green tops, chopped
1/2	cup chopped, tightly packed, washed fresh spinach
1	medium unpeeled red or white potato, cut into 1-inch cubes (about 1 1/2 cups)
1	medium tomato, chopped
1	small celery stalk, finely sliced (about 3/4 cup) (optional)
1/2	medium green bell pepper, seeded and chopped (optional)
1/2	cup chopped fresh cilantro (optional)
2	large cloves garlic, chopped
1	teaspoon olive oil
2	teaspoons ground cumin
1/4	teaspoon salt
	Lemon juice (optional)

1. Bring the lentils and water to a boil in a medium-size pot. Reduce the heat to simmer. Cover and cook for 30 minutes. Meanwhile, prepare the vegetables.

2. Add the vegetables, garlic, and oil. Cover and continue simmering the soup for 20 minutes. Add the cumin and salt and cook for a few more minutes, or until the vegetables are tender.

3. Serve immediately with a splash of lemon juice if you desire.

Yield: 3 servings

Kale and Potato Soup

PREPARATION TIME: 8 minutes
COOKING TIME: 35 minutes

Making soup doesn't get any simpler than this. If you want to have a dinner party, but you're low on money, kale soup is an economical meal. You can feed six friends for about $2.00. If you are not having a party, don't let the amount of soup this recipe makes stop you. It's delicious for breakfast, lunch, and dinner. One cup of cooked kale has almost as much calcium as one glass of milk.

1 bunch of kale, washed (about 3/4 pound)
2 pounds white potatoes (about 6 medium)
8 cups water
1 teaspoon salt
Olive oil (optional)

1. Wash the kale and remove and discard the tough stems. A big mound of curly greens will remain. Don't worry about having too much kale—as the leaves cook, they shrink dramatically. Crumple the leaves together in a pile, and slice them into about 1-inch-wide strips.

2. Wash the potatoes. Cut the potatoes in half lengthwise, and then slice the halves into 1/4-inch pieces.

3. Put the water and kale into a large pot. Bring the water to a boil and reduce the heat to medium. Cover the pot and cook for 10 minutes. Add the potatoes and salt. Cover and continue cooking until the kale and potatoes are tender, another 10 to 15 minutes. (The liquid should cook at a bubbling simmer.) Serve with a splash of olive oil if you desire.

Yield: 6 servings

Beer Stew

PREPARATION TIME: 12 minutes
COOKING TIME: 15 minutes

This is a flexible recipe. Adjust the amounts to suit your taste.

4   to 5 cups water
3   cups red potatoes, cut into 1/2-inch chunks (3 medium)
2   teaspoons olive oil
1   cup carrot, cut into 1/4-inch slices (about 1 medium)
1/2 cup chopped onion (about 1/2 small)
1   cup canned garbanzo beans, drained
1   teaspoon curry powder
1   cup dark ale or stout beer (about 1/2 bottle)
1/4 cup frozen peas
     Salt and pepper

1. Bring the water to boil in a medium saucepan. Add the potatoes and cook until just tender, but not mushy, about 10 minutes. Drain.

2. While the potatoes cook, heat the oil in a skillet over medium heat. Add the carrot, onion, and garbanzo beans; sauté 5 to 7 minutes over medium heat, stirring frequently.

3. Drain the potatoes and add them to the vegetable mixture. Add the curry and 1/2 cup of the beer. Simmer, uncovered, for about 3 minutes. Add the remaining 1/2 cup beer and simmer another 3 minutes to allow the alcohol in the beer to boil off, leaving its flavor essence in the pot. Remove from heat and stir in the peas. Salt and pepper to taste. Serve immediately.

Yield: 2 servings

Kale Vegetable Medley

PREPARATION TIME: 12 minutes
COOKING TIME: 15 minutes

This tasty combination satisfies the hearty appetite.

2	large white or red potatoes
1	cup firmly packed kale leaves, without stems
1	teaspoon olive oil
1/2	cup chopped onion (about 1/2 small)
1	clove garlic, chopped
1/2	teaspoon dried thyme
1	small tomato, chopped
1/2	cup canned white beans, rinsed and drained
	Salt and pepper

1. Wash the potatoes and cut them into 1/2-inch pieces. Add the water to a steamer pot or a pot with a steamer basket, keeping the water level lower than the bottom of the steamer. Cover the pot, and bring the water to a boil. Add the potatoes and steam for about 10 minutes, or until the potatoes are barely tender.

2. While the potatoes steam, wash the kale and remove and discard the hard stems. Gather the leaves into a pile, and hold them together with one hand while you cut the kale into about 1-inch slices. When the potatoes are done, remove the pot from the heat and uncover it. Set the potatoes aside.

3. Heat the oil in a medium nonstick skillet over medium heat. Add the onion, garlic, and thyme; sauté, stirring frequently for about 3 minutes or until the onion softens and becomes translucent. Add the kale and tomato, and sauté for 1 to 2 minutes, stirring until the kale has wilted. Add the potatoes and beans and heat for a minute or two. Salt and pepper to taste. Serve immediately.

Yield: 1 to 2 servings

Moroccan Stew

PREPARATION TIME: 12 minutes
COOKING TIME: 25 minutes

Serve this fragrant stew on a bed of warm couscous. If the ingredient list looks long, don't worry. The stew goes together in minutes.

2	teaspoons olive oil
3/4	cup chopped onion (about 1/2 medium)
1 1/2	cups thinly sliced cabbage
1/8	teaspoon salt
1/2	large green bell pepper or 1/2 cup zucchini cut into strips
1/8	teaspoon ground cinnamon
1	(14-ounce) can tomatoes, undrained and chopped
3/4	cup canned garbanzo beans, drained (about 8 ounces)
1/4	cup raisins
2	teaspoons fresh lemon juice
	Salt and pepper

1. Heat the oil in a medium nonstick skillet on medium heat and sauté the onion for 5 minutes. Add the cabbage and sprinkle with salt. Continue to sauté the vegetables for 5 to 6 minutes, stirring occasionally.

2. Add the bell pepper and cinnamon and sauté for 2 minutes. Stir in the tomatoes, garbanzos, and raisins. Cover and simmer for about 15 minutes.

3. Add the lemon juice. Salt and pepper to taste, and serve.

Yield: 2 servings

CHAPTER 6

Salads and Dressings

You can practically live on salads, and there are plenty of substantial combinations to choose from here. When you mix greens, beans, and grains, you have the makings for one-dish meals. With very little preparation, you can reproduce the expensive salads found in supermarket deli cases at a fraction of the cost.

Orange Rice and Black Bean Salad combines oranges and walnuts for a surprising flavor. Pasta Salad with black beans and vegetables can easily fill the center of any plate. Middle Eastern Traditional Tabbouleh Salad is a must-have in your vegetarian repertoire.

Leafy green salads present a special problem. While washed lettuce is tempting, dirty lettuce shrivels in the refrigerator. If washing and drying lettuce will put a stop to your salad making, treat yourself to prewashed, packaged salad greens. They may cost more, but they are worth the price.

Pasta Salad

Preparation Time: 5 minutes
Cooking Time: 6 minutes

Choose your favorite vegetables for this salad.

1	cup uncooked spiral pasta
1	cup broccoli florets
1/2	cup frozen corn, thawed
1	cup canned black beans, washed and drained
1	small tomato, chopped (about 1/2 cup)
	Parmesan cheese, grated (optional)
	Avocado slices (optional)

1. Cook the pasta, uncovered, in a pot of rapidly boiling water until it is "al dente" (cooked with a little "tooth" or crunch), 7 to 10 minutes. Just before you drain the pasta, toss in the broccoli and cook for no more than 1 minute. Drain the pot in a colander and rinse with cool water. This stops the cooking process and keeps the vegetables crisp-tender. (When making pasta salad, the noodles are rinsed, but do not rinse noodles when making hot pasta with sauce.)

2. Combine the salad ingredients in a medium bowl.

3. Dress with your favorite Italian dressing, or use one of the dressing recipes starting on page 86. Serve garnished with grated Parmesan cheese or avocado slices if you desire.

Yield: 2 servings

One Potato,
Two Potato Salad

PREPARATION TIME: 6 minutes
COOKING TIME: 12 minutes

This hearty salad sparkles with color and is a meal in itself.

4	cups water
1	cup red potato, cut into bite-size pieces
1	cup yam, peeled and cut into bite-size pieces
1	cup loosely packed, prewashed fresh spinach
6	peeled cucumber slices, about 1/8 inch thick
3	Greek olives (optional)
1	to 2 tablespoons fresh lemon juice or vinaigrette dressing
	Salt and pepper

1. Bring the water to a boil in a medium saucepan. Add the potato and yam and cook in rapidly boiling water until tender but not mushy, about 7 minutes. Drain thoroughly.

2. Arrange the spinach on a plate. Top with the cooked potato and yam, cucumber slices, and olives. Squeeze fresh lemon juice over the salad or dress with your favorite vinaigrette. Season to taste with salt and pepper.

Yield: 1 serving

Fruit Salad

PREPARATION TIME: 6 minutes

If you are tired of chomping on apples, try making a fruit salad. Once you get the hang of it, you can make a beautiful multifruit salad in minutes. Use firm apples and pears. Peel only if necessary. Squeeze a little lemon juice onto the cut pieces—without the citrus, they turn brown. Garnish with bananas just before serving. That way the bananas remain firm. You'll have a hard time keeping your housemates from snacking on any fruit salad left in the refrigerator.

1   apple, cored and chopped
1   pear, cored and chopped
1   tablespoon lemon juice
1   orange, peeled and chopped
     Banana slices
     Yogurt (optional)
     Nuts or raisins (optional)

1. In a bowl, gently mix the apple and pear with the lemon juice. Add the chopped orange and gently stir.

2. Spoon into a serving bowl and garnish with slices of banana. If you desire, top the salad with yogurt and a sprinkle of nuts or raisins.

Yield: 3 to 4 servings

Cabbage Slaw

Preparation Time: 6 minutes

Humble cabbage is one of the most versatile and underrated salad ingredients. The tart yogurt is a nice contrast to the sweet fruit. This is a fine fall salad when apples and pears are luscious.

1	cup shredded green cabbage
1/2	firm ripe pear, peeled and diced
1/2	apple, diced
1/4	cup raisins

Dressing

1/4	cup plain yogurt
1	teaspoon frozen orange juice concentrate
1	teaspoon honey

1. In a medium bowl, combine the cabbage, pear, apple, and raisins.
2. In a small bowl, combine all the dressing ingredients. Pour the dressing over the cabbage mixture, and gently toss. Serve with a thick slice of multigrain bread if you wish.

Yield: 1 serving

Green Salad with Oranges

PREPARATION TIME: 6 minutes

This good-to-eat salad is especially satisfying when citrus fruits are inexpensive and tomatoes cost a small fortune. It looks great, and it's a snap to prepare.

2   cups romaine lettuce, washed and dried
1/2   large orange, peeled and cut into bite-size pieces
1   tablespoon finely chopped red onion
       Honey-Yogurt Dressing (page 88)
       Salt and pepper

Tear the greens into bite-size pieces and arrange them on a plate. Top with the oranges, and sprinkle with the red onion. Splash with the dressing, and season with salt and pepper to taste.

Yield: 1 serving

Apple Raisin Couscous

PREPARATION TIME: 7 minutes

Couscous is finely cracked wheat that has been steamed, dried, and refined to some extent. This grain can be ready for eating in 5 minutes, and it can be the center of a multitude of salad creations. You'll find it in the grocery store shelved near the rice. This recipe uses apple juice to soften the grain, but hot water will also work. Eat the salad straight from a bowl, or serve it over a bed of lettuce.

1	cup apple juice
2/3	cup couscous
1/4	cup raisins
1/4	cup cooked garbanzo beans
1/2	medium apple, chopped (about 1/2 cup)
1/8	teaspoon ground cinnamon
3	cups lettuce, torn into bite-size pieces (optional)

1. In a small sauce pan, bring the apple juice to a boil. Stir in the couscous and raisins, and cover the pan. Remove the pan from the heat and let the couscous rest for 5 minutes, then fluff the couscous with a fork.

2. Add the garbanzo beans, chopped apple, and cinnamon. Serve over a bed of lettuce if desired.

Yield: 2 servings

Traditional Tabbouleh Salad

PREPARATION TIME: 6 minutes
SOAKING TIME: 15 to 20 minutes

Bulgur wheat is grain that has already been partially cooked and cracked into small pieces. It is prepared by pouring boiling water over the grain and letting it stand. You'll find bulgur wheat in the supermarket shelved near the rice. This salad happily accepts variations. If you like carrots, grate some and toss them in. Are you passionate about broccoli? Steam a few florets until crisp-tender and add them to your salad. Do you love juicy cucumbers? Chop a 1/4 cup and sprinkle it into the bowl, or pitch in a few garbanzo beans. If all that sounds like too much work, simply use the following recipe as is. It's delicious.

3/4	cup boiling water
1/2	cup cracked bulgur wheat
1	tomato, finely chopped
2	scallions, finely chopped (use whole scallions, greens and all)
1	clove garlic, minced
1/4	cup finely chopped fresh parsley
1/4	teaspoon dried mint
2	tablespoons fresh lemon juice
1/2	teaspoon olive oil
	Feta cheese (optional)
	Salt and pepper

1. Bring the water to a boil in a medium saucepan. Add the cracked bulgur wheat, cover, and remove the pan from the heat. Let the pot stand for 15 to 20 minutes. The bulgur will become soft and fluffy.

2. When the bulgur has absorbed the water, spoon it into a medium bowl and add the tomatoes, scallions, garlic, parsley, mint, lemon juice, and olive oil.

3. If you wish, sprinkle with feta cheese just before serving. Taste and season with salt and pepper. The salad will taste best if it sits in the refrigerator for 30 minutes before serving to let the flavors mingle. If you're too hungry to wait, go for it!

Yield: 2 servings

Marinated Vegetables

PREPARATION TIME: 5 minutes
COOKING TIME: 1 to 1 1/2 minutes

Marinated vegetables make satisfying snacks. They're great tossed into salads, piled on slices of bread, or eaten straight from the jar. Before placing vegetables in a marinade, first lightly steam them. Mushrooms, red onions, cucumbers, and cooked beans do not need presteaming. Marinated vegetables need to relax in the sauce for several hours before they're ready to eat. They will keep up to a week refrigerated in a tightly closed container, but they'll probably disappear long before that.

2	cups vegetables (carrots, broccoli, cauliflower, green beans, bell peppers)
1/4	cup canned garbanzo or kidney beans, drained
1	to 2 teaspoons olive oil
1/4	cup apple cider vinegar, wine vinegar, or balsamic vinegar
1	clove garlic, minced
1/4	teaspoon dried basil

1. Place the vegetables in a steamer over boiling water. Cover and steam 1 to 1 1/2 minutes, or until the vegetables are crisp-tender but not mushy.

2. Remove from heat and quickly cool the vegetables under cold water for about 30 seconds.

3. Place the vegetables and beans in a container; add the oil, vinegar, garlic, and basil. Cover the container with a tight fitting lid. Refrigerate. Rotate the container from time to time to evenly coat the vegetables.

Yield: 2 1/4 cups

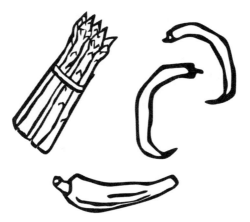

Buttery Bean Salad

PREPARATION TIME: 5 minutes

This speedy salad is prepared in a matter of minutes, and there is no lettuce to wash. Buttery lima beans dressed with fresh lemon juice and olive oil make a filling meal. Serve with a crusty slice of French bread and relax.

1	(15-ounce) can baby green or regular-size lima beans, drained (about 1 1/2 cups)
1/2	medium tomato, chopped
1	scallion, finely chopped
2	tablespoons finely chopped fresh parsley
	Juice of 1/2 lemon
2	teaspoons olive oil
	Salt and pepper
	Parmesan cheese (optional)

1. In a medium bowl, combine the beans, tomato, scallion, parsley, lemon juice, and oil. Gently toss.
2. Season with salt and pepper and a sprinkle of Parmesan cheese if desired.

Yield: 2 servings

Orange Rice
and Black Bean Salad

PREPARATION TIME: 6 minutes

*Here is a way to turn cooked rice and canned black beans into a
light, elegant meal.*

1/2 cup canned black beans, drained
3/4 cup cooked brown rice
1/2 cup finely chopped celery (about 1 stalk)
1/2 cup peeled and sliced orange (1 small or 1/2 large)
1/4 cup chopped scallion (about 1 medium)
1   tablespoon chopped fresh cilantro
     Salt and pepper
1   tablespoon chopped walnuts (optional)

Dressing
1/4 cup orange juice
1   tablespoon cider or balsamic vinegar
1/2 teaspoon olive oil
1/4 teaspoon ground cinnamon

1. In a medium bowl, combine the beans, rice, celery, orange,
   scallion, and cilantro.

2. In a small bowl, combine the orange juice, vinegar, oil, and
   cinnamon.

3. Pour the dressing over the rice salad and stir thoroughly.
   Season with salt and pepper. Garnish with the chopped
   walnuts, if you desire.

Yield: 1 serving

White Bean
and Tomato Salad

PREPARATION TIME: 6 minutes

A rustic salad full of traditional flavor. The white beans give this salad a creamy, satisfying taste.

1	(15-ounce) can white beans
2	scallions, finely chopped
1	clove garlic, minced
1	celery stalk, thinly sliced
1	medium tomato, chopped
1	tablespoon fresh lemon juice
1/4	teaspoon dried basil
1/2	teaspoon olive oil
	Salt and pepper
	Pinch of red pepper flakes (optional)

1. Rinse the beans gently in a colander. Drain.
2. In a medium bowl, combine the beans, scallions, garlic, celery, tomato, lemon juice, basil, and olive oil. Gently mix.
3. Salt and pepper to taste. Sprinkle with red pepper flakes if you desire.

Yield: 2 servings

Pineapple-Orange Yogurt

PREPARATION TIME: **4 minutes**

This fruit salad is also a good topping for pancakes and French toast.

1   cup vanilla yogurt
1/4   cup raisins
1/2   cup unsweetened pineapple chunks, drained
1   small orange, peeled and sectioned

Combine all the ingredients in a medium bowl. Spoon into a serving dish and eat.

Yield: 2 servings

Taco Salad

PREPARATION TIME: 8 minutes
COOKING TIME: 5 minutes

If you don't feel like washing lettuce, make the salad anyway and forget the greens. This salad is too good to miss. Don't let the long ingredient list scare you. The salad takes only minutes to prepare.

1	teaspoon vegetable oil
1	cup frozen corn
1	tablespoon water
1	teaspoon ground cumin
1	medium avocado, sliced
1	tablespoon lemon or lime juice
1/2	medium tomato, chopped
2	tablespoons chopped scallion (1 scallion with greens)
2	cups salad greens, torn into bite-size pieces
	Salt
	Baked tortilla chips, crumbled
1	tablespoon chopped fresh cilantro
	Tabasco sauce (optional)

1. In a small saucepan combine the oil, corn, water, and cumin. Cover and cook on medium heat for 3 minutes. Uncover and cook for 1 or 2 minutes to evaporate the excess moisture. Set aside.

2. Slice the avocado in half lengthwise. Remove the seed. Cut lengthwise and crosswise slices in the flesh making a grid pattern. Scoop the avocado cubes out of the shells and into a medium bowl. Gently stir in the lemon juice. Add the corn mixture, tomato, and scallion.

3. Spoon the salad onto a bed of greens. Salt to taste. Crumble a handful of baked tortilla chips and sprinkle them on top of the salad. Toss on the cilantro and a shake of Tabasco if desired. Serve and enjoy!

Yield: 2 servings

Downtown Salad

This salad couldn't be simpler. Select your favorite ingredients from the following list, and compose a salad on a big plate. Pour on your favorite dressing and dig in.

Romaine or Boston lettuce, washed, dried, and torn into bite-size pieces
Slivered red cabbage slices
Fresh spinach
Sprouts (alfalfa or mung bean)
Avocado slices
Tomato slices
Shredded carrots
Sliced beets
Bell pepper slices
Sliced celery
Frozen green peas, thawed
Green beans, steamed crisp-tender
Snow peas
Sliced scallion or red onion rings
Toasted nuts or seeds (cashews, sunflower, or sesame seeds)
Cooked garbanzo beans or kidney beans
Sautéed tofu
Sliced fresh mushrooms

Avocado and Pear Salad

PREPARATION TIME: 6 minutes

This simple, very green salad makes a light meal served with a slice of multigrain bread.

	Romaine lettuce (4 large leaves or 3 to 4 lightly filled cups)
1	ripe avocado
1	medium-ripe pear, cored, peeled, and diced
1	tablespoon fresh lemon juice
	Salt

1. Wash and dry the lettuce. Tear it into bite-size pieces and pile the lettuce onto individual plates.
2. Slice the avocado in half lengthwise, and gently twist to remove the seed. Make lengthwise and crosswise cuts into the flesh every 1/2 inch. Scoop the avocado cubes out of the shells. Place the avocado and pear in a medium bowl. Sprinkle with the lemon juice and gently stir.
3. Mound the pear and avocado mixture onto the lettuce leaves. Salt to taste.

Yield: 2 servings

Salad Dressing with Savoir Faire

There are many good bottled salad dressings on the market. If you have the time, you can make your own, but don't think salad dressing is any old vegetable oil and a $.59 bottle of vinegar. To make a salad worth eating, you absolutely need to have a good dressing. Choose a quality oil such as extra-virgin olive oil. A good vinegar is also essential; balsamic vinegar or mellow wine vinegar are good choices. Pick balsamic vinegar carefully and try different brands. There can be a big difference in flavor between the taste of pricey brands and budget brands.

The Basics

For foolproof dressing, always add a little salt, pepper, and garlic to your basic oil and vinegar. Most people also like some sweetener: Honey always works (just don't overdo it), and the taste of pure maple syrup will amaze you. These additions blend the sharper flavors of the dressing so that it tastes smoother to the tongue.

Dried herbs are fine for cooked food, but they are not strong enough for dressings (unless the dressing sits at least several hours). With a little extra cost and effort, you can make dressing sublime with fresh herbs. You can't go wrong with basil. Other good flavors include the tart sweetness of lemon, orange, and berry juices, or a sharp hint of mustard or horseradish. If you love creamy dressing, add a small amount of lowfat soft cheese, pureed silken tofu, or nonfat plain yogurt. Dressings will keep at least a week in the refrigerator in a tightly sealed container or jar, and the taste improves as the flavors merge.

Classic Vinaigrette Dressing

PREPARATION TIME: 3 minutes

1	tablespoon olive oil
3	tablespoons balsamic or wine vinegar
3	tablespoons lemon juice
2	cloves garlic, minced
1/8	teaspoon dried basil
	Salt and pepper

Whisk the ingredients together in a small bowl. Store in a covered jar in the refrigerator. It will keep for about 2 weeks.

Yield: About 1/2 cup

Honey-Yogurt Dressing

<small>PREPARATION TIME:</small> 3 minutes

Use this sweet, creamy dressing on fruit salads.

1/3	cup plain yogurt
1	teaspoon honey
1/8	teaspoon vanilla
2	teaspoons orange juice concentrate (optional)

Combine the ingredients in a small bowl. If tightly covered and refrigerated, it will keep for about a week.

Yield: About 1/2 cup

Creamy Garlic Dressing

<small>PREPARATION TIME:</small> 3 minutes

This dressing is also a tasty topping for baked or steamed potatoes.

1/2   cup plain yogurt
1   teaspoon Dijon mustard
2   cloves garlic, peeled and finely chopped
2   scallions, finely chopped
      Salt and pepper

Whisk together the ingredients in a small bowl. If tightly covered and refrigerated, it will keep for about a week.

Yield: About 1/2 cup

Sweet Mustard Vinaigrette

PREPARATION TIME: 3 minutes

2	tablespoons cider vinegar
2	tablespoons Dijon mustard
2	tablespoons maple syrup or honey
1/3	cup olive oil
	Salt

In a small bowl, whisk together the vinegar and mustard. Continue stirring while drizzling in the maple syrup and then the oil, until well blended. Add salt to taste. If tightly covered and refrigerated, it will keep at least 2 weeks.

Yield: About 2/3 cup

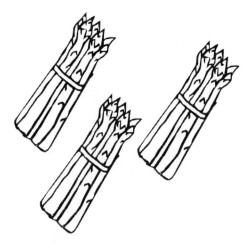

CHAPTER 7

Fast Foods—
Vegetarian Style
Sandwiches, Tortilla Wraps, and Pizzas

Sandwiches are a reliable mainstay for quick meals, and broadly defined, you'll find them popping up from around the globe in a variety of forms. Enjoy a warm Middle Eastern falafel sandwich tucked into Greek pita bread, a Broiled Eggplant Sandwich on crusty French bread, a creamy Green Chile Quesadilla on a crisp Mexican corn tortilla, or a versatile Italian pizza. If you're into burgers, you will be pleasantly surprised by the juicy Cremini Mushroom Burger you'll find in this chapter.

Chapati with Confetti Salad

Preparation Time: 5 minutes

Chapatis are India's daily flatbread. They're thin, soft, and pliable. If you can't find chapatis in the supermarket, whole wheat flour tortillas will work. This colorful sandwich is so delicious you might want to start by making two.

1	whole wheat chapati (or whole wheat flour tortilla)
1/3	cup hummus (recipe on page 48)
1/4	cup finely chopped red cabbage
1/4	cup finely chopped carrot
1/4	cup sprouts
1	teaspoon minced onion or scallion
1	teaspoon chopped black olives

1. Spread the chapati with a generous layer of hummus. Next, sprinkle with the cabbage, carrot, sprouts, onion, and olives.

2. Roll up the chapati jelly-roll fashion, and take a big bite.

Yield: 1 serving

Beyond Beef Sandwich

If you're accustomed to eating meat in a sandwich, this sandwich may sound like a non-idea. Give it a try. With all the trimmings, you'll never miss the animal.

2 slices multigrain bread
Mustard
Tomato slices
Lettuce
Red onion rings
Cucumber slices
Avocado slices
Alfalfa sprouts

Spread one slice of bread with mustard. Layer the bread with tomato, lettuce, onion rings, cucumber, avocado, and sprouts if you desire. Top with second slice of bread.

Yield: 1 sandwich

Cremini Mushroom Burger

PREPARATION TIME: 10 minutes

*A mushroom doesn't need to be psychedelic to expand your aware-
ness, and vegetarians need never apologize for their mushroom
burger. Pick your favorite burger bun or slices of crusty French
bread and 4 cremini mushrooms. (Creminis are those little brown
mushrooms sold in nearly every vegetable department.)*

*You can turn a basic burger into your taste fantasy by altering
the condiments. Instead of mustard, try pesto, barbecue sauce, or
horseradish—just don't try them all together. Choose your favorite
garnishes, and pile them on: lettuce, tomato, sliced red onion, marinated artichoke hearts, or roasted red peppers.*

4   sliced cremini mushrooms (about 1 1/2 cups)
1   to 2 teaspoons olive oil
1   large clove garlic, minced
1   teaspoon wine or water (optional)
1   burger bun or 2 slices French bread
     Salt and pepper

1. To clean the mushrooms, gently dust them off with a soft,
   damp paper towel.

2. Cut the mushrooms into 1/4-inch slices. Heat the oil in a
   nonstick skillet over medium-high heat, and sauté the
   mushrooms and garlic, stirring often. Cook for 6 to 7 minutes, or until the mushrooms are tender and shiny. It may

be necessary to reduce the heat to medium if the mushrooms are cooking too quickly, so watch the skillet. If the skillet becomes dry, add 1 teaspoon of wine or water to complete the sauté.

3. Layer the bread with mushrooms, and add your choice of condiments and garnishes. Salt and pepper to taste, and top with a second slice of bread. Then, lean over your plate and take a juicy bite.

Yield: 1 serving

Falafel

PREPARATION TIME: 15 minutes

Falafel is a spicy Middle Eastern pancake made from garbanzo beans. You can buy ready-made falafel mixes, but their taste or texture doesn't compare with falafel made from scratch. Stuff falafel into warm pocket bread with lettuce, tomato, and Tsiziki Sauce, a garlicky yogurt dressing (page 89). Here is a simple recipe for making these sumptuous pancakes without a mix. If there are extras, they won't last long. You don't need a food processor for this recipe—a masher or fork works fine.

1/2	medium red potato
1	teaspoon vegetable oil
1	small onion, finely chopped
1	can (15 1/2 ounces) garbanzo beans, drained
3	tablespoons fresh lemon juice (about 1/2 large lemon)
2	cloves garlic, minced
2	tablespoons tahini
1/2	teaspoon paprika (optional)
1	tablespoon finely chopped fresh parsley
	Salt and pepper
	Lettuce, tomato, Tsiziki Sauce (optional)

Preheat the oven to 350 degrees F.

1. Cut the potato into 1-inch chunks. Place the potato in a small saucepan with enough water to cover; boil until it is tender, about 10 minutes. Drain. While the potato cooks, heat the oil in a nonstick skillet over medium or medium-low heat and slowly sauté the onion until it is soft, stirring frequently, 8 to 10 minutes.

2. In a medium bowl, mash the garbanzo beans, potato, and lemon juice. Add the onion, garlic, tahini, paprika, parsley, and salt and pepper to taste; stir to combine. It will have a consistency similar to cookie dough.

3. Lightly oil a baking sheet with vegetable oil. Spoon the mixture onto the baking sheet, forming 3-inch pancakes. Place in the oven and bake for 15 minutes. Serve the falafel in a warm pocket bread, garnished with lettuce, tomato, and Tsiziki Sauce. Yum!

Yield: 6 servings; 12 (3-inch) pancakes

Broiled Zucchini Parmesan

PREPARATION TIME: 10 minutes

What you see is what you get in this open-face sandwich.

1	teaspoon olive oil
1/4	cup minced onion
1	clove garlic, minced
1	cup grated or thinly sliced zucchini
1/4	teaspoon dried basil
1/4	teaspoon dried oregano
	Tomato slices (3 or 4)
2	slices multigrain bread
1	tablespoon grated Parmesan cheese
	Pepper

1. Heat the oil in a nonstick skillet over medium heat. Sauté the onion and garlic until the onion is soft, about 3 minutes. Add the zucchini, basil, and oregano and continue cooking until it softens, about 3 minutes.

2. Layer half of the vegetables and tomato slices on each slice of bread. Lightly sprinkle with Parmesan cheese.

3. Broil for 1 minute or until the cheese melts. Pepper to taste. Eat with a knife and fork.

Yield: 1 serving

Curry in a Hurry

PREPARATION TIME: 10 minutes

This recipe makes enough filling for 2 pocket halves. Corn, sweet peppers, and curry deliver a delicious warm flavor.

1/2   teaspoon olive oil
1/4   cup chopped scallion (about 2 scallions)
1/4   green bell pepper (about 1/4 cup)
1/4   teaspoon curry powder
1/3   cup frozen corn
1/2   medium tomato, chopped
      Salt and pepper
1   pocket bread, cut in half

1. Heat the oil in a small nonstick skillet on medium heat and sauté the scallion and bell pepper for about 2 minutes. Stir in the curry, corn, and tomato and cook for 3 to 5 minutes, stirring. Remove from the heat; salt and pepper to taste.

2. Scoop the filling into warm pocket bread halves.

Yield: 2 servings

Broiled Eggplant Sandwich

PREPARATION TIME: 6 minutes
COOKING TIME: About 20 minutes

Filling, fast, and easy—everything you could want in a sandwich. Eggplant can be bland and boring or luscious and exciting. This sandwich is the latter. A purple eggplant sitting in the refrigerator is a lot friendlier sight than a big stick of bologna or salami. To cut an eggplant, first cut away any soft spots or blemishes on the part you plan to use and peel off a strip of skin where you will be making a crosswise cut. The knife is less likely to slip because it doesn't need to pierce the skin.

Marinade
1/4   cup water
1   teaspoon soy sauce
1   clove garlic, minced
1   teaspoon balsamic or wine vinegar
1   teaspoon olive oil

Filling
2   (1/2-inch-thick) eggplant slices
2   (1/4-inch-thick) tomato slices
    Pepper
4   slices French or multigrain bread
    Dijon mustard, pesto, or feta cheese
    Onion slices

Preheat the broiler.

1. In a small bowl, mix together the marinade ingredients.

2. Arrange eggplant slices on a lightly oiled baking sheet. Spoon about 2 teaspoons of the marinade onto each eggplant slice. Broil 3 to 4 inches from the heat for 3 to 4 minutes. Turn the slices over and spoon on more marinade. Broil another 3 minutes.

3. Remove the eggplant from the oven. Reduce the oven heat to 350 degrees F. Lay the tomato on top of the eggplant and sprinkle with pepper to taste. Bake on the middle rack of the oven for 15 to 20 minutes, or until the interior of the eggplant is soft. The purple shell is edible, and it might be slightly chewy. If you desire, remove and discard the cooked shell. Spread two slices of bread with mustard, pesto, or feta cheese. Layer each sandwich with the cooked eggplant and tomato. Top with onion slices and a second slice of bread.

Yield: 1 serving (2 sandwiches)

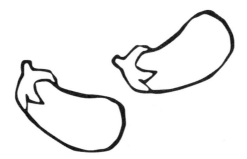

Crostini with a Bean and a Green

PREPARATION TIME: 10 minutes
COOKING TIME: 10 minutes

Italian crostini, literally "toast," is best made with crusty Italian or French bread, but any toasted bread will work. This version of crostini is covered with a creamy white bean spread mixed with greens.

1	can (16 ounces) white beans (1 1/2 cups)
2	tablespoons water
1	teaspoon olive oil
1	large clove garlic, minced
2 1/2	cups washed, tightly packed kale leaves without stems, finely chopped
2	tablespoons fresh lemon juice
	Salt and pepper
	Slices of toasted French or Italian bread

1. Wash and drain the beans and warm them in a saucepan with the water. Remove from the heat and coarsely mash the beans with a large spoon.

2. Heat the oil in a medium nonstick skillet over medium heat. Add the garlic and sauté for a few seconds; add the kale and stir. Cook, stirring frequently until it is tender and bright green, 7 to 10 minutes. The water that clings to the kale from washing is usually sufficient moisture for cooking. If the kale appears to be too dry, add water to the skillet one tablespoon at a time as necessary and continue sautéing.

3. When the kale is done cooking, add it, along with the lemon juice, salt, and pepper to the beans. Stir and taste. Add more salt and pepper if necessary. Spread the bean mixture onto the warm toasted bread for an open-faced sandwich, or use the toasted bread like you would chips and eat the spread as a dip.

NOTE: If you like the sharp taste of uncooked garlic, add it to the beans when you add the lemon juice.

Yield: 2 servings

Broiled Tofu

PREPARATION TIME: 5 minutes
TOFU PRESSING TIME: 30 minutes
COOKING TIME: About 10 minutes

Straight out of the box, tofu is a lot like pizza without a topping. But with a little planning, tofu might become your favorite fast food. Pressed tofu broils beautifully and tastes delicious. Pile broiled tofu onto a sandwich with your favorite toppings: mustard, relish, sliced onion, catsup, tomatoes, and crisp greens. It's so good you may find you've eaten it before there's time to build a sandwich. Make your own marinade or use hoisin sauce (available in well-stocked supermarkets and Asian markets). While the tofu is pressing, you'll have time to do a load of laundry.

1   block extra-firm or firm Chinese tofu (packaged in tubs of water)
    Prepared hoisin sauce or marinade

Marinade
3   tablespoons balsamic vinegar
3   tablespoons soy sauce
2   teaspoons catsup

1. To press the tofu, sandwich the tofu between two plates. Weigh the top plate with a heavy book, and press for 30 minutes. Remove the weight and top plate, and empty the water from the bottom plate. The tofu is now ready.

2. Preheat the broiler. Slice the pressed tofu into thirds length-wise. Place the tofu on a lightly oiled baking sheet and spread the tofu with the marinade.

3. Broil the tofu 3 to 4 inches from the heat for 5 to 7 minutes on each side, until browned and crisp on the edges. Serve it straight from the oven or make a tofu sandwich on toasted multigrain bread topped with your favorite condiments.

Yield: 2 servings

Pita with Creamy Zucchini

PREPARATION TIME: 7 minutes
COOKING TIME: 5 minutes

Here is a simple shredded zucchini sandwich lightly flavored with yogurt and a hint of mint. Shredded vegetables have a wonderful texture and look great on top of pizza, inside tacos, or simply eaten straight from the pan. This version is tucked into a pita bread.

1	medium zucchini, shredded
1	teaspoon olive oil
1	large clove garlic, minced
1/4	teaspoon dried mint
1/2	teaspoon dried oregano
1	tablespoon plain nonfat yogurt
	Salt and pepper
1	whole wheat pita bread, split in half

1. Shred the zucchini on the coarse side of a handheld grater with the largest holes.

2. In a medium nonstick skillet, heat the oil over medium heat. Sauté the garlic, zucchini, mint, and oregano, stirring often, until the zucchini is firm-tender and bright green, about 5 minutes.

3. Remove from the heat; stir in the yogurt. Season with salt and pepper. Scoop the filling into the warm pocket bread halves. Mmm . . . this is a satisfying meal!

Yield: 1 serving

Garlic Bread with Attitude

PREPARATION TIME: 3 minutes

This method uses raw garlic, so the flavor will be sharp and biting.

1   or 2 slices toasted bread
    Olive oil (optional)
1   clove garlic, peeled

Preheat the broiler.

1. Lightly brush or drizzle the bread with olive oil and toast it under a broiler 3 to 4 inches from the heat. (It is good without the oil, too.) Watch closely because the bread will brown quickly.

2. Rub the toasted bread with the peeled garlic.

Yield: 1 serving

Tortilla Wraps

Before you toss a package of tortillas into your shopping cart, read the nutrition label because the ingredients vary greatly from brand to brand. The list for corn tortillas should be short: corn, lime, and water. Check out the number of fat grams on flour tortillas, and choose tortillas with the smallest number. (Some have zero fat, but their texture can be rubbery.) Also, look for refrigerated wheat or flour tortillas free of preservatives. If you live in a community where freshly made tortillas are available, buy them; they're heavenly. Store all tortillas in the refrigerator or freezer. If you freeze them to use one at a time, let the tortilla thaw for a few minutes before cooking. Then, when the tortilla is warmed, it will toast and become crispy rather than steam and turn soggy.

Green Chile Quesadilla

PREPARATION TIME: 8 minutes

2   (6-inch or 8-inch) wheat or corn tortillas
1/4   cup vegetarian canned refried beans
2   tablespoons canned, diced mild green chiles
1/4   cup grated mozzarella cheese
1   tablespoon finely chopped fresh cilantro
     Prepared salsa

1. Spread half of the beans and chiles on one half of each tortilla. Sprinkle the cheese and cilantro onto the filling.
2. Warm a dry nonstick skillet on medium heat. Heat each tortilla in the skillet. When the tortilla becomes pliable, fold the plain half of the tortilla over the filling and cook each side for about 2 minutes, or until the cheese melts.
3. Serve with prepared salsa.

Yield: 1 serving (2 quesadillas)

Black Bean
and Yam Quesadilla

Preparation Time: 20 minutes

Black beans and yams combine for striking flavor and color in this hearty tortilla wrap.

1   teaspoon vegetable oil
1/2   cup finely chopped onion (about 1/2 medium)
1   clove garlic, finely chopped
1   teaspoon ground cumin
2   teaspoons water
1   cup peeled grated yam (about 1/2 medium)
1/4   cup black beans, rinsed and drained
       Salt and pepper
2   (8-inch or 10-inch) corn or wheat tortillas
1/4   cup grated Monterey Jack or mozzarella cheese
       Prepared salsa

1. Heat the oil in a medium nonstick skillet over medium heat. Add the onion and garlic and sauté for 3 minutes or until the onion is soft. Add the cumin and water and continue to sauté for 1 minute, stirring. Add the yam and beans, stir; cover and cook for about 6 minutes or until the yam is tender but not mushy. Remove the skillet from the heat. Season with salt and pepper.

2. When the skillet is cool enough to handle, wipe it with a paper towel. Reheat the skillet on medium heat. Place the quesadilla in the skillet and cook for a moment to soften the tortilla if necessary. Fold the tortilla in half and cook each side for about 2 minutes, until the cheese melts and the filling is warm.

3. Serve with prepared salsa.

Yield: 1 serving (2 quesadillas)

Tacos Monterey

PREPARATION TIME: 10 minutes
COOKING TIME: 15 minutes

The distinctive smoky flavor in these unusual tacos comes from chipotle peppers. These chiles are very tasty and very hot. You'll find small cans of chipotle chiles packed in adobo sauce in the Mexican section of the supermarket. (Mashed potatoes in a warm tortilla are delicious even without chipotle peppers. Add grated cheese and salsa to your taco instead.)

2	cups red or white potatoes, cut into 1/2-inch pieces (about 2 medium)
1/4	cup soy milk or dairy milk
1	canned chipotle pepper, finely chopped
	Salt
4	(6-inch) corn tortillas

1. Place the potato pieces in a saucepan with enough water to cover; boil until tender, 10 to 15 minutes. Drain. Pour in the milk and mash the potatoes with a strong fork or masher until they are smooth and creamy. Add more milk if necessary. Stir in the chipotle pepper. Taste. If you like food really hot, add one more chopped chipotle. Season with salt to taste.

2. Heat a tortilla on a hot, nonstick skillet over medium heat. The tortilla should be lightly toasted and flexible. Remove the tortilla from the skillet and spread about 1/4 cup of the potato mixture down the center. Fold the tortilla around the

filling, and take a bite. Add more oil to the skillet if necessary, and cook the remaining tortillas.

NOTE: Freeze the remaining chipotle chiles for future meals. Spread the peppers out on a dinner plate so that they do not touch each other. Place the plate in the freezer for about 30 minutes. Next, put the frozen chiles into a plastic container, and store the container in the freezer. Now it will be easy to use the chiles one or two at a time.

Yield: 1 serving

Spicy Zucchini Quesadilla

PREPARATION TIME: 8 minutes

Jalapeño peppers are an inexpensive culinary trick that add bright flavor to cooking. A little pepper costs about $.03.

1/2   teaspoon olive oil
1/2   medium zucchini, thinly sliced (about 1 cup)
1/2   jalapeño pepper (about 2 inches long), seeded, deveined, and finely chopped
2   (8-inch or 10-inch) wheat or corn tortillas
1   tomato (4 to 6 thin slices)
1   tablespoon chopped fresh cilantro or parsley
      Grated mozzarella cheese, Monterey Jack, or feta cheese (1 to 2 tablespoons per quesadilla)
      Prepared salsa

1. Heat the oil in a medium nonstick skillet on medium heat. Add the zucchini and jalapeño; sauté until the zucchini is tender, about 5 minutes. Stir occasionally.

2. Layer the zucchini mixture on one half of each tortilla. Add the tomato slices, cilantro, and cheese on top of the zucchini. When the skillet is cool enough to handle, wipe it with a paper towel. Reheat the skillet on medium heat. Place the quesadilla in the skillet, and when the tortilla becomes pliable, fold the plain half of the tortilla over the filling. Cook each side for about 2 minutes or until the cheese melts and the filling is hot. Cook the remaining quesadilla.

Yield: 1 serving (2 quesadillas)

Taco

1   (8-inch or 10-inch) corn tortilla

Choose any of the following:
Chopped fresh tomato
Fresh lettuce, torn into bite-size pieces
Sliced avocado
Cooked brown rice
Sliced olives
Chopped onions or scallions
Grated cheese: Monterey Jack, Cheddar
Plain yogurt
Chopped fresh cilantro
Chopped green bell peppers
Diced canned mild green chiles
Leftover sweet potato
Warm refried beans
Salsa

Heat a tortilla on a hot dry skillet and when it's pliable in about 30 seconds, fold the shell in half. Lightly toast both sides and remove from the heat. Stuff the tortilla with your favorite fillings.

Yield: 1 taco

Hot Lips Fajita

Fold a warm tortilla around sizzling sautéed vegetables, and you have a fabulous fajita. Jalapeño peppers fire up this version. If you have two skillets, use one to heat the tortilla while you quickly sauté the vegetables, or roll up the tortilla in a damp paper towel and warm it in a microwave for 25 seconds on High. If you have only one skillet, follow the directions in this recipe for heating the tortilla.

1/2	teaspoon vegetable oil
1	cup chopped zucchini (1 small)
1/2	cup broccoli (about 6 florets)
1/4	cup chopped and seeded red bell pepper (about 1/4 pepper)
1/2	jalapeño pepper, seeded and minced (about 2 inches long)
1/4	cup corn kernels (frozen or fresh)
1/4	teaspoon ground cumin
2	(10-inch) flour tortillas
1/4	cup shredded Monterey Jack or soy cheese

1. Heat the oil in a medium nonstick skillet over medium heat. Add all of the ingredients except the cheese and tortillas. Sauté the vegetables and cumin for 2 to 3 minutes, just until the vegetables begin to soften. Stir occasionally and make sure you don't overcook them. Remove the vegetables from the skillet. When the skillet is cool enough to handle, wipe it with a paper towel.

2. Reheat the skillet over medium heat. Place the tortilla in the skillet to warm, and spoon on half of the vegetable mixture and half of the cheese. Heat for about 1 minute, just until cheese begins to melt.

3. Remove the tortilla from the skillet. Sprinkle with chopped red onion if you desire. Fold up one edge of the tortilla, and wrap the two opposite sides of the tortilla around the vegetables and cheese. Take a bite from the open end.

Yield: 2 servings

Pizza—The Original Floppy Disk

One of the best parts about making pizza at home is that you're freed from trying to recycle the unwieldy cardboard box that never fits into the trash bin. Traditional ungarnished Italian pizza is made with a crust, tomato sauce, and melted cheese, but you can toss on just about anything that will withstand a 400 degree F heat. A 4-ounce can of tomato sauce flavored with 1 teaspoon of oregano makes a fine pizza sauce. You can use: English muffins, Italian focaccia, Boboli, bagels, French bread, or store-bought fresh or frozen pizza dough. Unless you love extra-thick pizza crust, cut Boboli bread in half to create two rounds of pizza or buy thin-crust Boboli.

The following recipes use pita bread for the base. There is enough topping for two 6-inch pizzas. When you choose a larger pizza crust, increase the topping amounts.

Pita Pizza Crust

1   (6-inch) pita bread

Preheat the oven to 450 degrees F.

Lightly toast the pita bread for 3 minutes in the oven. Remove the pita from the oven. If you like thin crust pizza, carefully split the pita bread around its outer edge to yield two equal rounds. If you like a thicker crust pizza, use the pita whole.

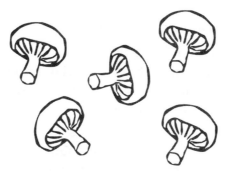

Pepper and Mushroom Pizza

PREPARATION TIME: 12 minutes

1	teaspoon olive oil
1/4	cup chopped onion, (about 1/4 medium)
1/2	cup chopped bell pepper (about 1/2)
1 1/2	cups sliced mushrooms (about 6)
1/4	teaspoon dried basil
1	(6-inch) pita bread
6	thin tomato slices
	Grated mozzarella cheese

Preheat the oven to 450 degrees F.

1. Heat the oil in a nonstick skillet over medium heat. Add the onion, bell pepper, mushrooms, and basil; sauté, stirring frequently for 3 minutes, or until the vegetables begin to soften. Remove from the heat.

2. Lightly toast the pita bread for 3 minutes in the oven. Remove the pita from the oven. Carefully split the pita bread around its outer edge to yield two equal rounds.

3. Spoon the filling onto the crust. Add tomato slices and lightly sprinkle with grated mozzarella cheese. Heat the pizza in the oven until the tomatoes are warm and the cheese begins to melt, about 2 minutes. Serve immediately.

Yield: 2 servings

Vegan Farmhouse Pizza

PREPARATION TIME: 12 minutes

$1/2$ teaspoon olive oil
$1/4$ cup diced onion
$1/2$ cup chopped apple (about $1/2$)
1   cup prewashed fresh spinach, tightly packed and then chopped
1   (6-inch) pita bread
$1/2$ teaspoon Dijon mustard
1   teaspoon chopped walnuts

Preheat the oven to 450 degrees F.

1. Heat the oil in a medium nonstick skillet on medium-high heat. Sauté the onion for 3 minutes. Add the apple and spinach; cook until the spinach wilts, 3 to 5 minutes. Press out excess moisture.

2. Lightly toast the pita in the oven for 3 minutes. Remove the pita from the oven and lower the heat to 350 degrees F. Carefully slice it in half around its outer edge to yield two equal rounds.

3. In a bowl, combine the spinach mixture and mustard. Spread the topping onto the toasted pita bread. Sprinkle with the walnuts and warm in the oven for about 5 minutes.

Yield: 2 servings

Roasted Vegetable Pizza

PREPARATION TIME: 7 minutes
COOKING TIME: 20 minutes

1   medium red potato, cut in half and then cut into
       1/4-inch slices
1   small zucchini, cut into 1/4-inch slices (about 1 cup)
1/3   medium bell pepper, coarsely chopped
1/2   cup coarsely chopped onion (about 1/2 small)
1   large clove garlic, minced
1   teaspoon olive oil
1/2   teaspoon dried thyme
1   (6-inch) pita bread
       Grated Parmesan cheese

Preheat the oven to 425 degrees F.

1. Place the vegetables in a medium bowl. Add the oil and thyme and stir to evenly coat the vegetables with oil. Spread the vegetable mixture onto a baking sheet. Don't crowd them or they'll steam—not roast. Bake for about 20 minutes, or until the potatoes are tender. Stir once or twice to ensure even cooking. Remove from the oven. Raise the oven heat to 450 degrees F.

2. Lightly toast the pita bread for 3 minutes in the oven. Remove the pita from the oven. Carefully split the pita bread around its outer edge to yield two equal rounds.

3. Spoon the filling onto the crust. If you desire, sprinkle each pizza with 1 or 2 teaspoons of grated Parmesan cheese and heat in the oven just until the cheese begins to melt. Serve immediately.

Yield: 2 servings

Zucchini and Cheese Pizza

<small>PREPARATION TIME:</small> 10 minutes

1	teaspoon olive oil
1/4	cup finely chopped onion
1/4	teaspoon dried basil
1	small zucchini, grated (about 1 cup)
1/2	cup chopped tomato
1	(6-inch) pita bread
	Grated Monterey Jack cheese
	Salt and pepper

Preheat the oven to 450 degrees F.

1. Heat the oil in a medium nonstick skillet over medium heat. Sauté the onion and basil for 3 minutes. Add the zucchini and cook, stirring frequently, for 2 minutes. Add the tomato, and cook for another minute. Remove from the heat.

2. Lightly toast the pita bread for 3 minutes in the oven. Remove the pita from the oven. Carefully split the pita bread around its outer edge to yield two equal rounds.

3. Spoon the filling onto the two crusts. Sprinkle with grated Monterey Jack cheese. Return the pizza to the oven and bake just until the cheese melts, 1 or 2 minutes. Season with salt and pepper.

Yield: 2 servings

Pizza Party

Don't let the fact that pizza is made from a yeast dough scare you off from making pizza from scratch. The scary part is the mess that accompanies pizza making. Until you are an expert dough handler, bits of dough wind up stuck all over the mixing area.

Making a big pizza at home can be expensive. Then why do it? It's fun, and when you make your own, it tastes better. An easy sauce can be made by simply opening a 4-ounce can of tomato sauce and adding $1/2$ teaspoon dried oregano or dried basil to enhance the flavor. Stir in a teaspoon of prepared pesto if you happen to have some.

Pizza doesn't have to be round. Just roll, stretch, and pat it into the shape of whatever baking pan you have. An empty beer bottle makes a good rolling pin. Lightly oil the baking pan before you add the dough. Keep cooking time short (20 minutes or less) when using cheese to prevent the cheese from becoming tough and rubbery. To cut the cost, consider having a potluck party, and ask your friends to bring a topping to add to the pizza. Enjoy!

Pizza Dough from Scratch

PREPARATION TIME: 60 minutes

Fast-rising yeast has this dough ready to roll, top, and bake in 60 minutes. The water you use to dissolve the yeast should feel warm to your hand. If it's too cold or boiling hot the yeast won't rise. Yeast likes a warm mixing bowl, so heat the bowl before you begin by filling it with warm water. In a minute or so, empty the water.

1	cup warm water (105 to 115 degrees F)
1	teaspoon sugar
1	package quick-rise yeast
1	tablespoon olive oil
$1/2$	teaspoon salt
1	cup whole wheat flour
2	cups all-purpose white flour

Preheat the oven to 400 degrees F.

1. In a large bowl, add the warm water, sugar, and yeast, stirring to dissolve. Let the mixture stand in a warm place for about 10 minutes or until it is bubbly.

2. Stir in the oil, salt, whole wheat flour, and $1^1/2$ cups white flour to form a stiff dough. Mix in the remaining $1/2$ cup white flour, a little at a time, until dough is easy to handle.

3. Turn the dough out onto a lightly floured surface and knead for 5 minutes, working in enough flour to make the dough smooth and elastic.

continued on next page

4. Wash and dry the mixing bowl. Then, lightly coat the bowl with oil. Place the dough in the warm, oiled bowl and turn it so the surface of the dough is oiled and the smooth side is up. Cover the bowl with a slightly damp dish towel. Set the bowl in a pie pan. Pour 2 cups of hot water into the pie pan. Place in a warm, draft-free place until the dough doubles in bulk, about 30 minutes.

5. Punch the dough down and divide into 2 equal-size balls for two small pizzas or use all of the dough for one large pizza. Roll and shape the dough. Place it in the baking pan and spread with sauce and toppings.

6. Bake pizza for about 15 minutes, or until dough is completely baked and toppings are cooked.

NOTE: You can top your homemade pizza dough with just about anything.

Fresh, sautéed, or lightly steamed:	Roasted Garlic	**Cheeses:**
Artichoke hearts	Roasted Peanuts	Cheddar
Bell peppers, green or red	Roasted Potatoes	Feta
	Rose Petals	Monterey Jack
Capers	Scallions	Mozzarella
Mushrooms	Sunflower seeds	Parmesan
Olives	Tomatoes	**Herbs, fresh or dried:**
Onions	Zucchini	
Parsley	**Lightly steamed:**	Basil
Pesto	Asparagus	Cilantro
Pineapple	Broccoli	Oregano
	Spinach	Rosemary

Yield: 1 large or 2 small pizza crusts

CHAPTER 8

Bean Meals

Beans are just about the perfect food. Eat them straight from the pot, wrapped in tortillas, tossed into soup, or made into dips. The quick route to eating beans is to buy them in cans. When you have time for soaking and simmering dried beans, a thrifty meal becomes dirt cheap.

Spilling the Beans—Gut Instincts

If you avoid eating beans because of fear of flatulence (gas), here's the good news. Beans contain sugars that humans cannot digest. When these sugars arrive in the large intestine, bacteria ferment them, producing gas. When beans become part of your regular diet, however, the body adapts and the intestinal problem disappears. People react differently to beans. If someone you know complains of discomfort after eating them, don't assume that will happen to you. If beans are new to your diet, eat them more frequently in small portions and avoid mixing beans in the same meal with other gas-producing vegetables, such as cabbage.

There are products on the market sold in natural food stores that help prevent the gas that beans cause. Beano is one brand name. Just add a few drops to your first bite.

Bean Cooking Chart

1 cup Dried Beans	Water (cups)	Cooking Time	Yield (cups)
Black	4	2 hours	2
Black-eyed peas	3	1 hour	2
Garbanzo	4	3 hours	4
Great Northern	$3^1/2$	2 hours	2
Kidney	3	$1^1/2$ hours	2
Lentils	3	45 minutes	$2^1/4$
Lima	3	$1^1/2$ hours	$1^1/4$
Navy	3	$2^1/2$ hours	2
Pinto	3	$2^1/2$ hours	2
Red	3	3 hours	2
Soy	4	$2^1/2$ hours	3
Split peas	3	45 minutes	$2^1/4$

Cooking Dried Beans

- Sort through dried beans. Pour the portion you are about to use onto a pan or dish. Run your fingers through them, and pick out any pebbles, twigs, or shriveled old beans you find. You will rarely find any, but it's worth looking. The last thing you want is a dentist's bill for a broken tooth from chomping on a rock. Pour the sorted beans into a colander and give them a quick rinse.

- Soften most dried beans by soaking them before cooking. If you don't soak beans, their skins will burst before they are tender. Because beans swell during this process, cover them with about twice their volume of water. Place the beans in a cool spot and soak them for 6 to 8 hours. (Softer beans such as lentils, split peas, and black-eyed peas do not need presoaking.)

- After soaking, drain the beans, and they're ready to cook. Add fresh water, cover the pot, and bring it to a boil. Then lower the heat and simmer until the beans are thoroughly cooked. Check periodically that the beans remain covered with water and replenish if necessary. Don't add salt until the beans have finished cooking or they may never become tender. Decrease the amount of salt needed by adding it at the end of the cooking process. When increasing a recipe, don't increase the seasonings as drastically as the main ingredients. Make small changes, and taste.

Chipotle-Black Bean Chili

PREPARATION TIME: 10 minutes

The chipotle chile pepper is the ingredient that gives this chili its deep flavor. You'll find chipotles in cans in the Mexican section of the supermarket. They come packed in adobo sauce, a very hot Mexican red sauce. A can of chipotle chiles goes a long way. It takes only 1 or 2 small chipotles to flavor a whole pot of chili.

1   teaspoon olive oil
1/2 cup chopped onion (about 1/2 small)
3   cloves garlic, minced
2   tablespoons chili powder
1   teaspoon minced canned chipotle pepper (1 chipotle)
2   (15-ounce) cans black beans, drained
2   (14 1/2-ounce) cans stewed whole tomatoes, undrained
     and chopped
1   (4 1/2-ounce) can chopped mild green chiles, drained
     Salt and pepper

1. Heat the oil over medium heat in a large saucepan or non-stick skillet. Add the onion and garlic, and sauté 3 to 5 minutes until the onion is tender; stir frequently. Add the remaining ingredients. Bring to a boil.

2. Reduce the heat, and simmer for 15 minutes. Ladle the chili into a bowl, and enjoy.

NOTE: Freeze remaining canned chipotle chiles for future meals.

Yield: 4 servings

Chili Uno-Dos-Tres

PREPARATION TIME: 10 minutes
COOKING TIME: 35 minutes

This chili has a lot of curb appeal; it looks and tastes great.

1	teaspoon olive oil
3/4	cup chopped onion (about 1 small)
3	cloves garlic, finely chopped
1/2	medium red or green bell pepper, diced (about 1/2 medium)
1	cup water
2	tablespoons chili powder
1 1/2	teaspoons ground cumin
1	(14 1/2-ounce) can ready-cut canned tomatoes, undrained
1	(15-ounce) can red kidney beans, drained
1	(15-ounce) can garbanzo beans, drained

1. Heat the oil in a skillet over medium heat. Add the onion, garlic, and bell pepper; sauté 5 to 7 minutes; stirring frequently.

2. Add the water, chili powder, cumin, tomatoes, kidney beans, and garbanzo beans. Bring to a boil. Reduce the heat; gently simmer, uncovered, for 30 minutes. Ladle into a bowl and serve with corn bread if you desire.

3. ¡Olé!

Yield: 2 to 3 servings

Black-Eyed Peas

PREPARATION TIME: 6 minutes
COOKING TIME: 45 to 55 minutes

Black-eyed peas are one of the few beans that can be cooked without presoaking. They'll cook in about the same amount of time, 45 to 55 minutes, and taste the same whether you soak them or not, but they won't look the same. When beans soak overnight, they slowly rehydrate and hold their shape throughout the cooking process. Without presoaking, a violent rehydration occurs, causing some of the skins to crack and separate from the beans. It sounds more murderous than it really is.

If you're out of onion and bell pepper, cooked black-eyed peas can stand on their own dressed with fresh lemon juice and a splash of olive oil. If you're in the mood for a simple-to-prepare, delicious meal, forget the soaking and start cooking.

2 cups dried black-eyed peas
1 small onion, finely chopped (about 1 cup)
1 medium bell pepper, chopped (about 1 cup)
1 teaspoon dried oregano

Toppings
Olive oil
Fresh lemon juice
Salt and pepper
Chopped tomato
Fresh cilantro

1. Cover the beans with fresh water; add the onion, bell pepper, and oregano. Bring the pot to a boil, and simmer until the beans are tender, 45 to 55 minutes. Keep the pot par-

tially covered at all times. Check the beans occasionally, and add more water if needed.

2. Remove the beans from the pot with a slotted spoon; dress them with a drizzle of olive oil, lemon juice, and salt and pepper to taste. If you're a garlic fanatic, mince some and toss it on, too.

3. Garnish with chopped tomato and cilantro.

NOTE: For variety, garnish the black-eyed peas with salsa, a splash of Tabasco sauce, or Vietnamese chili sauce. Black-eyed peas are also delicious spooned over cooked rice or added to soups.

If you choose to presoak the beans, here's how to do it. Cover the beans with twice their volume of water, and soak for 8 hours or overnight. Drain.

Yield: 4 servings

Dal

PREPARATION TIME: 10 minutes
COOKING TIME: About 30 minutes

This Indian soup-like dish is made with lentils. It's the Indian version of a stew, and the variations are endless. You'll find lentils in the supermarket near the dried beans. Lentils cook quickly and are easy to prepare. Garnish the dish with either sliced avocado, chopped fresh tomato, a dollop of yogurt, or a spoonful of chutney. If you're busy with studies and work, take a break and cook a batch. This one-pot dish makes a robust first meal or last meal of the day.

1	cup lentils
3	cups water
2	cups finely chopped onion (about 2 medium)
1	teaspoon olive oil
2	cloves garlic, finely chopped
1	teaspoon curry powder
	Salt

1. In a medium saucepan, combine the lentils, water, and 1 cup of onion. Bring the ingredients to a boil; reduce the heat, cover the pan, and simmer until the lentils are tender, about 30 minutes.

2. While the lentils are cooking, heat the oil in a nonstick skillet; add the remaining 1 cup onion, garlic, and curry. Sauté the vegetables on medium or medium-low heat, stirring occasionally until they are golden, soft, and just beginning to brown, 10 to 15 minutes.

3. Add the onion mixture to the cooked lentils, stirring to combine. Heat the lentil mixture for a few minutes longer. Salt to taste. Serve.

Yield: 4 servings

Easy Pot-o-Chili

PREPARATION TIME: 15 minutes
COOKING TIME: 60 to 90 minutes

Cook up a pot of chili and call your friends for a fiesta. Soak the beans for 6 to 8 hours before you plan to cook them, and allow about 1 hour for the beans to simmer. Serve with a splash of salsa and a dollop of yogurt if you desire. If you like really thick chili, add more cornmeal.

2   teaspoons vegetable oil
1   cup chopped onion (about 1 medium)
2   cloves garlic, finely chopped
1   cup dried beans, presoaked
     (small red beans or kidney beans)
1   (14-ounce) can diced tomatoes
2   tablespoons canned diced green chiles
1   tablespoon chili powder
1   teaspoon powdered cumin
1   tablespoon cornmeal
     Salt
     Salsa (optional)
     Yogurt (optional)

1. In a large pot, heat the oil and sauté the onion and garlic on medium to medium-low heat for 6 to 10 minutes or until tender.

2. Drain the beans. Add the beans to the pot with enough fresh water to cover. Bring the pot to a boil, then reduce the heat to low. Cover and simmer until the beans are tender, about 60 minutes. Check the pot occasionally to see that the beans remain covered with water.

3. When the beans are tender, add the tomatoes, green chiles, chili powder, cumin, and cornmeal. Taste and then season with salt. Gently simmer for another 10 to 15 minutes uncovered, stirring occasionally. Serve with a dollop of salsa or yogurt if desired.

Yield: 4 servings

Pete's Harbor Special

Prepared in a matter of minutes, this uncomplicated meal is full of flavor. It originated from a restaurant on the San Francisco Bay.

1   medium zucchini
1   teaspoon olive oil
1/2   teaspoon dried thyme
1   cup canned vegetarian refried beans
1   clove garlic, minced
       Salt and pepper
       Prepared salsa
       Grated mozzarella or Monterey Jack cheese (optional)

1. Wash and dry the zucchini. Cut off the ends. Next, cut the zucchini diagonally into long, oval-shaped 1/4-inch-thick slices.
2. Heat the oil in a medium nonstick skillet on medium-high heat. Add the zucchini and sprinkle with thyme. Quickly fry the zucchini slices until they are golden-speckled on both sides, about 10 minutes. Remove the zucchini from the pan.
3. Heat the beans and garlic in a small saucepan. Spread the beans in a thin layer onto a warm plate. Arrange the zucchini slices on the beans. Season with salt and pepper. Add a splash of salsa and a sprinkle of grated mozzarella or Monterey Jack cheese. (Place the plate in a warm oven on low heat for a minute or two to melt the cheese if you desire.)

Yield: 1 serving

Black Bean Quickie

PREPARATION TIME: 6 minutes

Here is a hearty meal without cooking. Eat this dish as a dip or make it into a sandwich. Great with baked tortilla chips, scooped into pocket bread, or spread onto crusty French bread.

1	(15-ounce) can black beans, drained
1	avocado
1/2	cup prepared Mexican-style red salsa
1	to 2 tablespoons chopped fresh parsley or cilantro
1/2	chopped medium tomato
	Salt and pepper

1. In a medium bowl, roughly mash the beans with a fork or masher.

2. Halve the avocado lengthwise and gently twist to separate it from the pit. Make lengthwise and crosswise cuts about 1/2 inch apart in the flesh of each half. Scoop the avocado cubes out of the skin, and add them to the beans. Stir in the salsa, parsley or cilantro, and chopped tomato. Salt and pepper to taste.

3. Serve as a dip or use as a sandwich spread.

Yield: About 2 cups

Marinated Tempeh

PREPARATION TIME: 15 minutes

Tempeh is a favorite Indonesian soy food made from fermented soybeans. Think of it as tofu's sibling. It has a chunkier texture and a bit more flavor than tofu. Like tofu, tempeh acts as a sponge, soaking up the flavors that surround it. If you are still struggling with the idea of giving up meat, tempeh has a very "meaty texture," and you can do anything to tempeh that you can do to meat. To keep tempeh fresh, store it in your refrigerator. It freezes well and keeps its flavor and texture for several months. You'll find tempeh widely available in natural food stores and even some supermarkets. If you notice a few dark spots on the tempeh when you open the package, that's normal. Eat this dish straight out of the frying pan or add it to soups, stews, salads, grains, chili, or filled tortillas. It's super simple to prepare and it's too good to miss.

2	ounces tempeh
1	tablespoon white or cider vinegar
1	tablespoon soy sauce
1 1/2	teaspoons water
1	large clove garlic, minced
1	teaspoon vegetable oil
	Pepper

1. Cut the tempeh into about 1/4-inch-thick strips or cubes and set aside. In a shallow bowl, stir together the vinegar, soy, water, and garlic.

2. Add the tempeh and stir it around a few times. Let it sit in the marinade for a few minutes to absorb the sauce.

3. In a nonstick skillet, heat oil on medium-high heat and sauté the tempeh for about 8 minutes until it is golden and crisp. If necessary, add a little more oil to prevent sticking. Pepper to taste and serve immediately.

NOTE: Tempeh can be easily cooked by broiling. Marinate the tempeh following the recipe directions. Lightly oil a baking dish, and broil the slices 3 to 4 inches from heat for 3 to 5 minutes on each side until lightly browned.

Yield: 1 serving

CHAPTER 9

Grain Meals

Whole grain cooking is one of the most enjoyable discoveries a new vegetarian can make. These unrefined foods are full of protein, vitamins, and minerals. Marketers design the ads you see for quick-cooking grains and rice cookers to make you think there is something mysterious and difficult about cooking grains. Once you become acquainted with them, they are surprisingly easy to prepare.

There are only two things that can go wrong: too much water or too little water, and that's easy to fix. If the grain is not tender at the end of the cooking time, add more water—just a little, 1/4 cup or less—and let the grain cook a little longer. If you added too much water, lift the cooked grain out of the pot with a slotted spoon, leaving the excess water behind. The grain may be soggy, but you can use less water next time.

Store uncooked grains, especially cornmeal, in the refrigerator or freezer. It doesn't take long for hungry insects to find a warm kitchen and begin feasting on staples of grain. They know a good thing when they find it.

Here's a selection of some favorite grains:

Couscous and Bulgur These owe part of their celebrated reputation to the fact that they're quick to prepare. Just pour boiling water over the grains, and they soften and are ready to eat in 10 to 20 minutes.

Rice   A sure crowd pleaser, but it takes a long time to cook brown rice. That can be a problem when you're hungry and in a hurry. One solution is to create deliberate leftovers by cooking more rice than you need for one meal. Cooked rice will keep refrigerated for a week, and you'll have a head start on future meals.

Polenta   One of the best ways imaginable to eat corn. Serve the polenta while it's soft and warm, or pour it into a baking pan or onto a plate and refrigerate it to eat later. As polenta cools, it becomes firm and ready for slicing. When you're ready to eat, cut the polenta into slices and heat it in a skillet, the oven, or the broiler. It will keep refrigerated for several days.

Rolled Oats   A bowl of hot oatmeal is delicious any time of the day. Old-fashioned rolled oats take about 15 minutes to cook, quick-cooking rolled oats cook in about 5 minutes, and instant oats are ready instantly. They all share the same high nutritional value, but instant oats are nearly always packaged with salt and sugar. Rolled oats and quick-cooking oats take so little time to prepare that you are much richer financially and nutritionally if you avoid instant oats.

Noodles   One of the most popular quick-cooking grains of all.

The Perfect Pot—of Grain, of Course

Here is a simplified guide for cooking grains. You may notice that a film clings to the side of the saucepan after removing the cooked grain. Fill the pot with water and let it rest for a while (30 minutes or overnight). Then the coating will practically slide off the pot by itself.

Bulgur   One cup of dry bulgur yields 2¹/₂ cups cooked. To prepare bulgur: Measure 1 cup of bulgur into a heat-proof bowl, and pour in 1 cup of boiling water. Cover the bowl, and set it aside for about 20 minutes. When the bulgur has absorbed the water, stir to fluff the grains. If it's still too chewy, add more hot water.

Couscous   One cup of couscous yields two cups cooked. Place equal amounts of boiling water and dry couscous in a heat-proof bowl. Cover tightly and let sit for about 5 minutes. Stir to fluff the grain. If it's still crunchy, add a small amount of hot water.

Old-Fashioned Rolled Oats   *Stove Top Cooking* To make 1 cup of oatmeal: Stir ¹/₂ cup of old-fashioned rolled oats into 1 cup of boiling water. Boil for 5 minutes, stirring occasionally. Cover, remove from heat, and let it stand for a few minutes before serving.
   Microwave Cooking To make 1 cup of oatmeal: Combine ¹/₂ cup of old-fashioned rolled oats and 1 cup of water in a 2 cup microwavable bowl. Microwave on Medium for 5 to 6 minutes, or until the oats have thickened. Mix well before serving.

Polenta (cornmeal)   The amount of water used in cooking polenta is not an exact science and can vary slightly depending on how "stiff" you want the mixture to be. If it's too dry, add more water. Polenta is extremely elastic. Mixing the cornmeal with a little water before adding it to the boiling water keeps it from becoming lumpy.
   Stove Top Cooking To make 2 cups of polenta: Combine ¹/₂ cup cornmeal and ¹/₂ cup water in a bowl. Bring 2 cups of

water to a boil in a medium saucepan. Stir in the polenta mixture. Reduce heat to the lowest setting, stirring continuously to prevent the polenta from sticking. Simmer on low for 10 minutes, or until the polenta is thick and creamy. If it becomes too stiff or dry while cooking, add a small amount of water (1 to 2 tablespoons at a time) and keep stirring.

Microwave Cooking To make 2 cups of polenta: In a 1-quart microwavable bowl, whisk together 1/2 cup cornmeal and 2 cups water. Cook in microwave on High for 3 minutes. Stir, then microwave on High for an additional 2 minutes. Remove the polenta from the microwave, and let it rest for 1 minute. The polenta should be the consistency of pudding. If it appears watery, microwave for an additional 1 to 2 minutes.

Brown Rice   One cup of raw brown rice yields 3 cups cooked. To cook 1 cup of raw brown rice, add 2 cups of water. To cook 2 cups of raw brown rice, add 4 cups of water. For greater quantities of rice, lower the proportion of water to rice—for example, for 3 cups of raw rice, use about 4 1/2 cups of water.

Cook rice in a pot with a tight-fitting lid. Using a dented lid or one that is the wrong size lets too much water escape during cooking. Rinse the rice and drain it, then add the proper amount of fresh cool water to the pot. Cover and bring to a boil over the highest heat. When steam escapes from below the lid, turn off the heat for 5 minutes. Return to very low heat and simmer for about 35 minutes or until the water has been absorbed. Remove from heat and let it sit, covered, for a few minutes before serving. Refrigerate cooked brown rice in a covered container. It will keep for about a week.

White Rice   Use 1 3/4 cups water for each cup of rice and prepare as for brown rice, without rinsing before you cook. The water should be absorbed in 15 to 20 minutes of cooking.

Reheating 1 cup of cooked rice
- On top of the stove: Heat rice in a covered saucepan on medium heat with 2 tablespoons of liquid for 4 to 5 minutes.
- In the oven: Put rice in a baking dish. Add 2 tablespoon of liquid and reheat in an oven set at 350 degrees F for 4 to 5 minutes.
- In a microwave, heat rice with 2 tablespoons of water. Cover the container; microwave on High 1 minute.
- Steaming: Place the rice in a steamer basket over boiling water: Cover and steam for 2 minutes or until the rice is warm.

Grain Cooking Chart

1 cup Grain	Water (cups)	Cooking Time (minutes)	Yield (cups)
Amaranth	3	25	2
Barley	3	45	$3^1/2$
Brown rice	2	45	3
Buckwheat	2	15	$2^1/2$
Kasha	2	15	$2^1/2$
Bulgur	2	15	$2^1/2$
Couscous	1	15	$2^3/4$
Millet	$2^3/4$	40	$3^1/2$
Quinoa	2	15	$2^1/2$
Wild rice	3	60	$2^2/3$

Spontaneous Couscous

PREPARATION TIME: 6 minutes
COOKING TIME: About 18 minutes

When liquid is added to this tiny mild-tasting grain, it magically puffs up and becomes tender in less than ten minutes. Here couscous is energized with frozen green peas, tomatoes, and onions. It makes a quick, light meal, or a great sandwich tucked into a warm pocket bread. If you desire, add Broiled Tofu just before serving (pages 104–105). Use about 2 cups of vegetables per serving and make substitutions at will. (Double the recipe and chill leftovers for a ready-made salad for tomorrow dressed with a vinaigrette dressing.)

1	teaspoon olive oil
1	cup chopped onion (1/2 medium)
1/2	cup frozen peas
1/2	medium tomato, chopped
1/4	cup couscous
1/2	cup water
1	teaspoon finely chopped fresh parsley (optional)
	Tabasco or fresh lemon juice (optional)
	Salt and pepper

1. Heat the oil in a medium nonstick skillet. Sauté the onion on medium-low heat for 10 minutes, or until the onions are lightly browned, stirring occasionally.

2. Add the peas, tomatoes, couscous, and water.

3. Cover and cook on low heat for 5 to 8 minutes, or until the peas are bright green, all the water is absorbed, and the couscous is soft. Add parsley.

4. Serve with a splash of Tabasco or fresh lemon juice if desired. Salt and pepper to taste.

Yield: 1 serving

Polenta with Mushroom Gravy

PREPARATION TIME: 15 minutes

This recipe is a two-part process, but it's straightforward and uncomplicated. You can have a lick-your-plate meal ready in 15 minutes.

Polenta

1/2   cup cornmeal

1 1/2   cups water

Gravy

1   tablespoon olive oil

1   cup chopped onions

1/2   teaspoon dried thyme

2   cups sliced fresh mushrooms (about 4 large)

1   tablespoon flour

2/3   cup water, or white wine, or red wine

1   tablespoon soy sauce

      Pepper

1. In a 1-quart microwave-safe bowl, whisk together the cornmeal and water. Cook in the microwave on High for 3 minutes. Whisk carefully (mixture will be hot); return the mixture to the microwave and cook 1 minute on High, or until the polenta is thick and creamy. Remove from the microwave and let the polenta rest while you cook the gravy.

2. Heat the oil in a small nonstick skillet on medium or medium-low heat. Sauté the onion and thyme for 6 min-

utes; stir occasionally. Add the mushrooms and continue to sauté on medium heat until the mushrooms soften, stirring often, for 3 to 5 minutes. If the skillet becomes dry before the mushrooms are soft, add 1 tablespoon of water and continue cooking.

3. When the mushrooms are soft, add the flour and stir for a moment, then add the water and soy sauce. Simmer on medium-high, stirring until the sauce thickens, about 30 seconds to 1 minute. Remove from the heat.

4. Serve the polenta topped with gravy. Pepper to taste.

NOTE: This gravy is delicious on mashed potatoes, rice, or noodles. If you choose to use water rather than wine, add 1 clove of finely chopped garlic when you add the mushrooms. Believe it or not, the water makes as tasty a gravy as the wine; they're just different.

Yield: 2 servings

Polenta with Black Beans

PREPARATION TIME: 15 to 20 minutes
COOKING TIME: 20 minutes

A mixture of cornmeal and water cooked as a mush is native to the Americas. The Italians adopted it as a staple of their cuisine and called it polenta. If you like pasta, you'll love polenta. It's the ultimate comfort food and it's versatile, nourishing, and cheap. Cooked polenta can be topped with pasta sauce, sautéed or steamed vegetables, or cooked beans. It is often used as a stuffing and can be broiled or fried. It's lovely sprinkled with grated cheese. Polenta makes a delicious alternative to potatoes or rice. In this recipe, polenta is made on the stove, but if you have a microwave, it's even faster. (See Polenta with Mushroom Gravy on page 150–151.)

1	teaspoon olive oil
$1/2$	cup chopped onion (about $1/2$ small)
2	cloves garlic, minced
1	teaspoon dried thyme
1	($14 1/2$-ounce) can diced or ready-cut tomatoes, undrained
1	(15-ounce) can black beans, rinsed and drained
$1/2$	cup cornmeal
2	cups water
	Grated Parmesan cheese
1	tablespoon chopped fresh parsley (optional)

1. Heat the oil in a medium nonstick skillet over medium heat. Add the onion, garlic, and thyme. Sauté on medium heat for 3 to 5 minutes, until the onion is tender. Add the tomatoes and beans. Reduce the heat to low and gently simmer the bean mixture while you prepare the polenta.

2. In a small bowl, combine the cornmeal and $1/2$ cup water. Set aside. In a medium saucepan, bring $1 1/2$ cups water to a boil; pour in the cornmeal mixture and stir; reduce the heat to its lowest setting. Cook, stirring frequently, until the mixture is thick and smooth, about 10 minutes. If the polenta sticks to the bottom of the pot, add more water, 1 tablespoon at a time.

3. Serve beans and polenta side by side. Sprinkle with Parmesan cheese and chopped parsley if you desire.

Yield: 2 to 3 servings

NOTE: If you don't have a microwave, use the stove-top method for cooking polenta on page 150.

Indian Rice

PREPARATION TIME: 12 minutes

1/2	teaspoon vegetable oil
1/2	medium onion, chopped
1/2	medium carrot, thinly sliced on diagonal
1/4	green pepper, chopped
1/4	teaspoon curry powder
1/4	cup crushed pineapple
1	cup cooked rice
1/2	ripe banana, sliced
1	tablespoon raisins
	Salt
1	tablespoon peanuts

1. Heat the oil in a nonstick skillet over medium heat. Sauté the onion and carrot for 3 minutes. Add the bell pepper and curry and sauté for another 2 minutes. Add the pineapple and rice; stir. Reduce the heat to low.

2. Gently stir in the banana and raisins being careful not to mash the bananas. Cook until the bananas are warm, 1 or 2 minutes.

3. Salt to taste. Sprinkle with the peanuts. Serve.

Yield: 1 serving

Chinese Fried Rice

PREPARATION TIME: 6 minutes
COOKING TIME: 3 to 4 minutes
MARINATING TIME: About 10 minutes

This recipe happily accepts substitutions. Use whatever vegetables you have on hand—broccoli, snow peas, or carrots are good choices.

2	tablespoons soy sauce
2	teaspoons sugar
1/4	block extra-firm tofu
1/4	teaspoon vegetable oil
1/4	cup red or green bell pepper, cut into thin strips (about 1/4 medium)
1	cup cooked rice
1/4	cup frozen peas
1/4	cup chopped scallions (about 1 scallion)

1. In a shallow bowl, mix together the soy sauce and sugar. Cut the tofu into strips about 1/2 inch wide. Marinate for about 10 minutes in the soy and sugar mixture.

2. Heat the oil in nonstick skillet over medium heat. Add the pepper, stir, and fry for 1 to 2 minutes. Remove the tofu from the marinade and add the tofu to the skillet. Stir for a moment. Add the rice and heat thoroughly, about 1 minute. Add the peas and scallions and stir.

3. Taste. If you desire, top the dish with some of the remaining marinade. Serve immediately.

Yield: 1 serving

Beer and Aztec Rice

PREPARATION TIME: 7 minutes
COOKING TIME: About 40 minutes

One of the best parts of this recipe is that you can drink the leftover beer. The ingredient list may look long, but the recipe is super simple, and the taste is fantastic.

1	tablespoon minced jalapeño (about $1/2$ medium)
$1/2$	cup finely chopped large onion (about $1/2$)
3	large cloves garlic, minced
$1 1/2$	teaspoons olive oil
1	tablespoon finely chopped fresh cilantro
$1 1/2$	teaspoons ground coriander
$1/2$	teaspoon ground cumin
1	cup brown rice
1	cup water
1	cup dark beer, ale, or stout
$1/4$	teaspoon salt
$1/2$	cup frozen peas, thawed

1. If you like food really hot, leave a few of the seeds in the jalapeño. If you like a mild flavor, remove the seeds and vein. In a medium saucepan, sauté the jalapeño, onion, and garlic in olive oil until the onion softens, about 5 minutes. Add the cilantro, coriander, and cumin and sauté about 1 minute.

2. Add the rice, water, beer, and salt. Bring the pot to a boil. Reduce the heat and cover. Cook on low heat for 35 to 40 minutes, until the rice is tender. If the rice is nearly done and the liquid is almost gone, turn off the heat and let the rice sit on the burner for another 5 minutes.

3. Remove the pot from heat and stir in the peas. Re-cover the pot and let it sit for 5 minutes to warm the peas. Serve.

Yield: 3 servings

Sicilian Rice

PREPARATION TIME: 12 minutes

1   cup canned diced tomatoes, drained
     (1/2 of a 15-ounce can)
2   teaspoons olive oil
1/2 onion, chopped (about 1/2 cup)
1   clove garlic, chopped
1 1/2 stalks celery, thinly sliced (about 1/2 cup)
1/2 bell pepper, diced (about 1/2 cup)
1/2 teaspoon dried thyme
1 1/2 cups cooked rice
     Salt and pepper

1. Drain the tomatoes, reserving the juice. Set aside.

2. Heat the oil in a medium skillet on medium heat. Add the onion and garlic and sauté until soft, about 5 minutes. Stir in the celery, bell pepper, and thyme; cook for 3 additional minutes.

3. Add the tomatoes, and gently stir in the rice. If the rice is dry, add some of the reserved tomato liquid. When the rice is hot and the liquid is absorbed, the dish is ready to serve. Season with salt and pepper to taste.

Yield: 2 servings

Rice with Garbanzo Beans

PREPARATION TIME: 10 minutes

Traditional Mediterranean flavors give a cup of rice great taste.

1	teaspoon olive oil
1/2	cup finely chopped onion
1	clove garlic, finely chopped
1	cup tightly packed, washed chopped spinach
1	tablespoon fresh lemon juice
1/4	cup garbanzo beans
1/2	medium tomato, chopped (about 1/2 cup)
1/2	teaspoon dried thyme
1	cup cooked rice
2	to 4 tablespoons crumbled feta cheese
	Salt and pepper

1. Heat the oil in a medium skillet over medium heat. Add the onion and garlic and sauté for about 3 minutes, until the onion softens.

2 Stir in the spinach, lemon juice, garbanzo beans, tomato, and thyme. Add rice, cover, and cook for 2 to 3 minutes, stirring occasionally.

3. When the spinach has wilted and the rice is hot, serve topped with crumbled feta cheese. Salt and pepper to taste.

Yield: 1 serving

Rice, Yams, and Greens

PREPARATION TIME: 10 minutes
COOKING TIME: About 60 minutes

Here is a hearty, wholesome, and easy three-course meal. What you don't eat now will be good for breakfast. By the time you finish eating the greens, the potato will be almost ready. By the time you're done with the potato, the rice will be ready, but you may be too full to eat any. Later, though, it will be tempting enough to keep you away from junk food.

1	cup brown rice
2	cups water
2	yams
2	to 3 cups prewashed spinach
	Balsamic vinegar or lemon juice
1/8	teaspoon nutmeg (optional)
	Salt and pepper

Preheat the oven to 450 degrees F.

1. In a medium saucepan, rinse and drain the rice. Add water to the pan, cover, and bring the rice and water to a boil. When steam escapes from below the lid, turn off the heat for 5 minutes. Return to very low heat and simmer for about 35 minutes or until the water is completely absorbed.

2. While the rice cooks, put the yams in a baking dish and bake for about 60 minutes until they are tender. (You can eat the skins if you wish.)

3. In a medium skillet or saucepan, steam the spinach in 1/4 inch of water until it is bright and tender, about 3 minutes. Drain the spinach and serve. Sprinkle with balsamic vinegar or lemon juice. Lightly dust with nutmeg if you desire. Salt and pepper to taste. Serve.

Yield: 2 servings

Rice Vera Cruz

PREPARATION TIME: 6 minutes
COOKING TIME: About 8 minutes

This dish can be the center of your meal or complement a bowl of chili.

2	teaspoons vegetable oil
1/4	cup frozen corn
1	teaspoon seeded and minced jalapeño
1/2	teaspoon ground cumin
1/2	medium tomato, diced
2	scallions, finely chopped
1	tablespoon finely chopped fresh cilantro
2	cups cooked rice
	Salt

1. In a medium nonstick skillet on medium heat, warm the oil. Add the corn, jalapeño, and cumin; cover and cook on low heat for 3 to 5 minutes, stirring occasionally.

2. Stir in the tomato, scallions, cilantro, and rice. Cook on low heat for 3 to 5 minutes until hot. Stir occasionally. Add a dash or two of water if needed to prevent the rice from sticking.

3. Salt to taste and serve.

Yield: 2 servings

CHAPTER 10

Pasta

There are dozens of different kinds and shapes of noodles from which to choose. When you are busy and overworked, noodles can become one of your best friends. The directions on packages of pasta usually overcook the noodles. Begin checking for doneness after about 5 minutes of cooking.

Cooking pasta is not much harder than boiling water. You can prepare some of the best toppings in the same amount of time it takes to cook the noodles. While ready-made pasta sauce straight from a jar is tasty, it becomes boring as a steady diet. The following recipes will make you a versatile pasta cook.

Super-Excellent Pasta

To make 1 serving of pasta, use about 4 ounces of noodles. Bring 3 quarts of water to a rapid boil. Make sure you have enough water in the pot to allow the pasta to swim freely while it cooks. Add the pasta to the boiling water. Stir once with a long-handled wooden spoon to keep the pieces from sticking together; cover the pot so that the water will quickly return to a boil. (If you taste-test pasta dangling from a wooden spoon, you won't burn your lips or tongue on a hot metal utensil.)

When the water boils, remove the lid and stir once again. Start testing for doneness after 5 minutes. For pasta served hot, cook it *al dente*, or just to the point where there is a slight resistance or "tooth" when you bite it. Drain cooked pasta immediately. Don't run cold water over it, because the outer layer of starch that remains helps the sauce stick.

Rice Noodles   You will find rice noodles in Asian markets and well-stocked natural food stores. They are great in clear soups, topped with your favorite pasta sauce, added to stir-fries, or in Thailand's best known noodle dish—pad thai. They're ready to eat in about 8 minutes.

Place the noodles in boiling water and boil for 5 minutes; add salt and continue boiling for an additional 2 to 3 minutes or until translucent. Drain and rinse in cold water.

Ramen Noodles   Heat and serve these precooked wheat noodles in just minutes. Use them in clear soups or as a foundation for sautéed vegetables or pasta sauce.

Pasta with Zucchini and Basil

PREPARATION TIME: 10 minutes
COOKING TIME: 12 minutes

Zucchini is a vegetable that has an affinity for pasta.

1/4	pound spaghetti
1	teaspoon olive oil
2	to 3 cloves garlic, finely chopped
1	small or 1/2 medium zucchini, sliced (about 1 cup)
1/4	teaspoon dried basil
	Salt and pepper
2	teaspoons fresh lemon juice
	Grated Parmesan cheese

1. Bring a covered pot of water to a rapid boil. Stir in the pasta and cover the pot until the water returns to a boil. Uncover and cook until the pasta is al dente (begin checking for doneness after about 5 minutes of cooking).

2. While the pasta cooks, heat the oil in a medium skillet over medium-high heat. Add the garlic, zucchini, and basil. Sprinkle lightly with salt and pepper. Quickly fry until the zucchini begins to brown, about 5 minutes, stirring occasionally. Add the lemon juice and stir. Remove from the heat.

3. When the pasta is al dente, drain it. Place the hot pasta on a warm plate; top with zucchini and grated Parmesan cheese. Lightly toss. Salt and pepper to taste.

Yield: 1 serving

Pasta with Green Beans and Feta Cheese

Preparation Time: 8 minutes
Cooking Time: 12 minutes

The classic flavors of green beans and feta cheese combine in this dish to make a truly simple, yet outstanding meal. Buy a bag of frozen green beans. It's easier to scoop out what you need from a bag than a cardboard box.

1/4	pound pasta
1	teaspoon olive oil
1/4	cup thinly sliced onion
1	large or 2 small cloves garlic, minced
1/8	teaspoon dried basil
1 1/2	cups frozen French-cut green beans
1/2	cup chopped tomato (1 medium)
	Crumbled feta cheese
	Salt and pepper

1. Bring a covered pot of water to a rapid boil, stir in the pasta, and cover until the water returns to a boil. Uncover the pot and cook the pasta until al dente, 8 to 10 minutes.

2. While the pasta cooks, heat the oil in a medium nonstick skillet over medium heat. Add the onion, garlic, and basil; sauté until the onion is soft, 3 to 4 minutes, stirring occasionally. Add the green beans and stir. Cover and cook on

medium-low heat until the beans are hot and crisp-tender, about 5 minutes. Just before you serve the beans, stir in the fresh tomato.

3. When the pasta is al dente, drain and serve topped with the green bean sauce. Sprinkle generously with feta cheese and season with salt and pepper to taste.

Yield: 1 serving

Farfalle and Peas

PREPARATION TIME: 10 minutes
COOKING TIME: 20 minutes

Farfalle is the Italian name for bow-tie pasta. The nooks and cran-nies in the bow-ties help hold the peas on your fork. The 15-minute onion sauté gives this simple dish great flavor.

1	teaspoon olive oil
1	cup chopped onion (about 1 small)
1	cup frozen peas
	Salt and pepper
2	cups uncooked bow-tie pasta
	Grated Parmesan cheese (optional)

1. Bring a covered pot of water to a rapid boil. While the water comes to a boil, heat the oil in a medium nonstick skillet over medium heat. Add the onion and lower the heat to medium-low; sauté for 10 to 15 minutes, stirring occasionally. (This long, slow sauté is what gives this dish its great flavor.) When the onion begins to turn brown, add the peas and salt and pepper to taste. Stir. Cook for 1 or 2 minutes. Cover and turn off the heat leaving the skillet on the burner while the pasta finishes cooking.

2. When the pot of water boils, stir in the pasta, and re-cover the pot for a moment until the water returns to a boil. Un-cover the pot. As soon as the pasta is cooked al dente (begin

checking for doneness after about 5 minutes), drain it. Bow-tie pasta may take a few minutes longer to cook than spaghetti.

3. Serve the pasta topped with the onion and peas. Sprinkle with Parmesan cheese if you desire. Salt and pepper to taste.

Yield: 1 serving

Pasta Primavera

PREPARATION TIME: 10 minutes
COOKING TIME: 10 minutes

Here is a pasta vegetable medley for two. Don't let the ingredient list scare you. It takes only 5 minutes to chop the vegetables.

1/2	pound spaghetti
1	teaspoon olive oil
1/2	cup chopped onion (about 1/2 medium)
1	clove garlic, minced
1/2	medium carrot, sliced
1/4	green bell pepper, chopped
4	mushrooms, sliced (about 1 cup)
1/2	cup zucchini, sliced (about 1 small or 1/2 medium)
1/4	teaspoon dried basil
1/8	teaspoon dried oregano
1/2	medium tomato, chopped
2	tablespoons water
2	to 4 teaspoons fresh lemon juice (optional)
	Grated Parmesan cheese
	Salt and pepper

1. Bring a covered pot of water to a rapid boil, stir in the pasta, and cover until the water returns to a boil. Uncover the pot and cook the pasta until al dente, 8 to 10 minutes.

2. While the pasta cooks, heat the oil in a medium nonstick skillet over medium heat. Add the onion, garlic, and carrot; sauté until the onion is soft, about 3 minutes. Add the green pepper, mushrooms, zucchini, basil, and oregano; sauté stirring occasionally until the vegetables begin to soften,

about 3 minutes. Add the tomato and 2 tablespoons of water; cover and cook for 3 minutes, or until the vegetables are just tender. Uncover, stir, and remove from the heat.

3. When the pasta is al dente, drain it. Serve the pasta topped with the vegetable mixture. Sprinkle each serving with a splash of fresh lemon juice and grated Parmesan cheese. Salt and pepper to taste.

Yield: 2 servings

Pasta Puttanesca

Preparation Time: 8 minutes
Cooking Time: 15 minutes

Capers are the pickled flower buds of a Mediterranean shrub with a sharp, distinctive flavor. You'll find them in the relish section of the supermarket. They're packed in brine, so rinse them before using, and store the rest of the jar in the refrigerator. (Capers are good sprinkled on pizza and tossed into pasta salad.)

1	medium tomato, chopped (about 1 cup)
2	cloves garlic, minced
2	teaspoons capers, rinsed and drained
1	tablespoon sliced black olives, drained
1/4	pound spaghetti
1	teaspoon olive oil
	Grated Parmesan cheese
1	teaspoon minced fresh parsley
	Salt and pepper

1. Bring a covered pot of water to a rapid boil. While the water heats, chop the tomato and garlic; drain the capers and olives. When the water comes to a rolling boil, stir in the pasta, re-cover the pot for a moment, and return it to a boil. Uncover the pot and cook the pasta to al dente (begin checking for doneness after about 5 minutes of cooking).

2. While the pasta cooks, heat the oil in a medium nonstick skillet on medium heat. Sauté the tomato and garlic for about 5 minutes, stirring occasionally. Add the capers and olives and lower the heat to the lowest setting, and continue cooking, stirring occasionally, for 1 to 2 minutes. Remove from the heat.

3. When the pasta is al dente, drain well and add the pasta to the tomato mixture. Gently stir and serve immediately. (The pasta is stirred into the sauce to ensure that none of the sauce is left behind in the skillet. This sauce is too good to miss even a drop.) Sprinkle with Parmesan cheese and parsley if you desire. Salt and pepper to taste.

Yield: 1 serving

Pasta with Garbanzo Beans

PREPARATION TIME: 12 minutes
COOKING TIME: 15 minutes

The buttery flavor of garbanzo beans makes rich-tasting pasta. If you're out of spinach, use a chopped fresh tomato instead. Either way, it's delicious.

1/4	pound spaghetti
1	teaspoon olive oil
1/2	cup chopped onion
1	large clove garlic, minced
1/2	teaspoon dried dill
2	cups tightly packed, chopped spinach
1/4	cup canned garbanzo beans, rinsed and drained
2	tablespoon fresh lemon juice
	Grated Parmesan cheese
	Salt and pepper

1. Bring a covered pot of water to a rapid boil. When the water comes to a rolling boil, stir in the pasta; re-cover the pot, and return it to a boil. Uncover the pot and cook the pasta al dente (begin checking for doneness after about 5 minutes of cooking).

2. Heat the oil in a medium nonstick skillet on medium heat. Sauté the onion, garlic, and dill for about 5 minutes, stirring occasionally until the onion softens. Add the spinach and

garbanzo beans and continue cooking, stirring until the spinach wilts, about 3 minutes.

3. When the pasta is al dente, drain it. Serve the pasta topped with the spinach mixture. Sprinkle with lemon juice and grated Parmesan cheese. Salt and pepper to taste.

Yield: 1 serving

Pasta with Greens

PREPARATION TIME: 8 minutes
COOKING TIME: About 10 minutes

Whip up this fabulous meal and enjoy the rich taste of tender greens and creamy cottage cheese tossed with pasta. You can substitute washed spinach in this recipe if you desire. (If you don't have kale, the pasta is just as tasty tossed with cottage cheese and chopped scallions.)

1/4	pound spaghetti
1	cup tightly packed washed kale (stems removed)
1	tablespoon water
1/2	cup nonfat cottage cheese
2	cloves garlic, minced
1	tablespoon chopped walnuts
	Salt and pepper

1. Bring a large covered pot of water to a rapid boil. Add the pasta, stir, and cover the pot until the water returns to a boil. Uncover the pot and continue cooking until the pasta is al dente (begin checking for doneness after about 5 minutes of cooking).

2. Finely chop the kale. When the pasta has cooked for about 4 minutes, add the kale and 1 tablespoon of water to a nonstick skillet on medium heat, cover, and cook until it is wilted and still bright green, 3 to 5 minutes. Turn off the heat and stir in the cottage cheese and garlic.

3. When the pasta is al dente, drain it, and serve it tossed with the kale mixture. Sprinkle with walnuts. Salt and pepper to taste.

   NOTE: If the kale stems are small, you may only need to discard the tough bottom portion.

Yield: 1 serving

Spaghetti Pancake

PREPARATION TIME: 10 minutes

Use up leftover pasta with this crispy noodle pancake. If you never have leftovers, it's good enough to make pasta especially for it.

1   teaspoon olive oil
1   to 2 cups cooked spaghetti
    Grated Parmesan cheese
    Salt and pepper
    Applesauce (optional)

1. Heat the oil in a nonstick skillet over medium heat.
2. Add the pasta and fry until the underside is brown and crispy, 6 to 8 minutes.
3. Serve sprinkled with Parmesan cheese and salt and pepper to taste, or top with a dollop of applesauce.

Yield: 1 serving

Peanut Pasta

Boil up a pot of pasta and choose a sauce. Either one of these sauces can be ready in minutes without any cooking. Peanut sauce is also good served over cooked rice, baked sweet potatoes, and a variety of steamed vegetables.

Pasta and Vegetables
1/4   pound spaghetti or linguini
1   cup broccoli florets
1/2   cup thinly sliced carrot (about 1/2 medium)
1   cup thinly sliced Chinese cabbage
1   tablespoon finely chopped scallion (about 1 small)

Peanut Sauce with Tahini
1   tablespoon peanut butter
1   tablespoon tahini
1   tablespoon apple cider vinegar
1   to 2 tablespoons orange juice
1   teaspoon soy sauce

Peanut Sauce with Salsa
2   tablespoons peanut butter
2   tablespoons fresh lemon juice
2   tablespoons prepared Mexican red salsa
1   teaspoon brown sugar
       Salt

1. Bring a covered pot of water to a rapid boil. While the water boils, choose one of the sauces and mix together the sauce ingredients in a small bowl until smooth and creamy. Add more juice if necessary.

2. When the water boils, stir in the pasta, re-cover the pot, and return it to a boil. Uncover the pot and cook until the noodles are al dente or just tender (begin checking for doneness after about 5 minutes of cooking).

3. While the noodles cook, steam the vegetables in a steamer basket placed in a pot or in a steamer. Add water to the pot and bring it to a boil, then add the broccoli and carrot; steam for 1 1/2 to 2 minutes. Add the cabbage; steam for another 30 seconds or until the vegetables are crisp-tender. Make sure the water does not touch the vegetables while they cook.

4. When pasta is al dente, drain it, and serve it immediately tossed with the vegetables and sauce. Garnish with chopped scallion.

Yield: 1 serving

CHAPTER 11

Various Vegetables, Stir-Fries, and Potato Dishes

Many of the vegetable dishes in this chapter are versatile enough to be a meal by themselves or to accompany other dishes. According to the book *Potatoes,* by Alvin and Virginia B. Silverstein, Frederick the Great of Prussia decreed in 1744 that anyone who refused to grow and eat potatoes would have their ears and nose cut off. You may not have time to grow potatoes, but you'll find great potato recipes and delicious vegetable meals in this chapter along with the how-to's of artichoke eating.

Artichoke Feast

PREPARATION TIME: 5 minutes
COOKING TIME: 30 to 40 minutes

If you are looking for an entertaining meal and you like eating with your fingers, this strange looking vegetable is for you. Cook the artichoke, and then just do what comes naturally. Pull off a leaf and dunk it in the sauce. (This is the traditional method, but an artichoke is good enough to eat without any dip.) Put the leaf in your mouth and pull it through your teeth, scraping off the tender flesh. Discard what's left, and pull off another leaf. A big pile of scraped leaves will accumulate on your plate. When you get to the center, scoop out and discard the thistle-like "choke." What's left under the choke is the soft "heart." It's the best part. Cut it into bite-size pieces and dunk it into the sauce. Tahini Dipping Sauce on page 44, or Tsiziki Sauce on page 43 are both excellent choices.

1   globe artichoke
2   tablespoons fresh lemon juice or wine vinegar
1   teaspoon olive oil
1   clove garlic

1. Cut off the stem of the artichoke so it will sit evenly on the bottom of a pot. Stand the artichoke up in the pot with 3 inches of water. Add the lemon juice or vinegar, oil, and garlic; cover the pot and bring it to a boil. Reduce the heat and

simmer until the stem end is tender or a leaf can be removed with the slightest resistance (30 to 40 minutes). Check the pot from time to time to see if the water has boiled away. Add more water if necessary.

2. When the artichoke is done, drain it well, and serve it on a plate with a bowl of sauce if you desire. Eat it hot, warm, or chilled.

Yield: 1 serving

Easy Asparagus

PREPARATION TIME: 5 minutes
COOKING TIME: About 20 minutes

Asparagus is a divine vegetable that arrives in the produce department in the spring. It is delicious to eat along with a sandwich or use it as a salad.

1/2   pound fresh asparagus
1   teaspoon olive oil
      Salt
2   cloves garlic, chopped
      Lemon juice

Preheat the oven to 400 degrees F.

1. Wash the asparagus and snap off the tough ends of the stalks. Hold the stalk with the thumb and index finger of both hands, and the woody part will break off naturally in the right spot.

2. Place the asparagus on a baking sheet and drizzle the olive oil over the spears. Sprinkle on some salt and roll the asparagus around until all of it is lightly coated with oil. Dot the spears with bits of chopped garlic.

3. Put the asparagus in the oven. Check after 10 minutes, and when the stalks are slightly blistered, turn them over. Total roasting time will vary depending on the thickness of the stalks. Cook until tender, 20 to 30 minutes. Serve sprinkled with a few drops of lemon juice.

NOTE: Asparagus can also be cooked by steaming over boiling water until tender-crisp. It will take 3 to 6 minutes, depending on the thickness of the stalks. Salt and pepper to taste and sprinkle with lemon juice, or dip the spears in Tsiziki Sauce (page 43) if you wish.

Yield: 1 to 2 servings

Steamed Vegetable Combo

PREPARATION TIME: 8 minutes

Great vegetarian eating doesn't get any easier than this. Steamed vegetables can be a stand-alone one-bowl meal eaten hot or cold, or they can be paired with a variety of other dishes. The trick to making them taste good is to avoid overcooking. Begin checking for doneness in 2 minutes. The vegetables should be crisp-tender when done. Chilled and dressed with a vinaigrette dressing, a splash of balsamic vinegar, or a squeeze of lemon juice, and you have a salad. Serve them hot, topped with creamy Tsiziki Sauce (page 43) or Tahini Dipping Sauce (page 44) if you wish.

$^1/_2$ cup sliced carrots, cut $^1/_2$ inch thick (1 carrot)
$^1/_2$ cup broccoli florets (1-inch pieces)
$^1/_2$ cup cauliflower florets (1-inch pieces)
   Salt and pepper

1. Arrange the vegetables in a steamer over boiling water.
2. Cover and steam 4 to 5 minutes or until crisp-tender.

Yield: 1 serving

Stuffed Acorn
Squash and Pears

PREPARATION TIME: 5 minutes
COOKING TIME: About 45 minutes

This fragrant meal is the spirit of the fall harvest.

1   acorn squash, split lengthwise and seeded
1/2   cup chopped pear
1   tablespoon undiluted orange juice concentrate
1   tablespoon brown sugar or honey
1/2   teaspoon cinnamon

Preheat the oven to 400 degrees F.

1. Place the squash cut-side up on a baking sheet. In a large
   bowl, combine the pear, orange juice concentrate, sugar,
   and cinnamon.

2. Spoon the mixture into the squash cavities.

3. Bake 45 minutes to 1 hour until the squash is soft.

Yield: 2 servings

Roasted Red Bell Pepper

PREPARATION TIME: 3 minutes
COOKING TIME: 8 to 15 minutes

Red bell peppers take on a whole new personality when roasted or slowly sautéed. Once you've discovered their sweet taste, they'll become a mainstay in your vegetarian eating. They are cheapest in the fall. Use them on sandwiches, crackers, cooked pasta, green salads, baked potatoes, stir-fries, and with cooked grains. Anywhere they land, they're luscious. You can either roast or sauté the pepper; each cooking method produces a special taste, and both are delicious. Eat the pepper now or store it in a covered container in the refrigerator. It will keep for a week.

1   red bell pepper
1   teaspoon olive oil

Preheat the broiler.

To Roast

1. Cut the pepper in half lengthwise. Discard the seeds and membranes. Place the pepper on a baking sheet with its shiny skin-side facing up. Broil 3 or 4 inches from the heat for 8 to 10 minutes or until the skin is blackened and charred.

2. Remove the pepper from the oven. Seal it in a paper bag to steam for 10 minutes. (It works even if you skip the paper bag trick.) Peel and discard the charred skin. Do not rinse; that will wash away the smoky taste. Slice roasted peppers into lengthwise strips. Drizzle with a little oil.

To Sauté
Cut the pepper in half lengthwise. Discard the seeds and membranes. Slice the pepper into lengthwise strips. Heat oil in a small nonstick skillet on medium heat. Sauté the pepper on medium or medium-low heat for 15 minutes, stirring frequently until tender and lightly browned.

Yield: Makes 1/2 cup

Gingered Chinese Greens Stir-Fry

PREPARATION TIME: 15 minutes
TOFU PRESSING TIME: 15 to 20 minutes

Serve this simple, crisp stir-fry over warm rice or cooked noodles. The chili oil called for in this recipe may also be labeled red oil, hot oil, or hot pepper oil.

1/2	cake Chinese-style firm tofu (about 7 ounces)
2	teaspoons vegetable oil
1/2	teaspoons minced or grated gingerroot
2	cups packed shredded Chinese cabbage or bok choy (4 or 5 leaves)
	Splash of chili oil
1	tablespoon finely chopped fresh cilantro

Sauce

1	tablespoon soy sauce
3	tablespoons orange juice
1	tablespoon fresh lemon or lime juice
1	tablespoon water
1	teaspoon sugar
1/2	teaspoon cornstarch

1. Sandwich the tofu between two plates. Top with a heavy book. Press for 15 to 20 minutes. Remove the weight and top cover, and drain the water from the bottom plate. The tofu is now ready to use. Cut the tofu into 1/2-inch cubes. Heat

1 teaspoon vegetable oil in a medium nonstick skillet on medium-high. Stir and fry the tofu until it is lightly browned, about 6 minutes. Remove from the heat and set aside.

2. In a small bowl, combine the sauce ingredients.

3. Re-oil the skillet with the remaining 1 teaspoon of oil. Heat the oil on medium-high heat. Stir in the ginger and add the greens; stir and fry until the greens begin to wilt, 2 to 3 minutes. Gently toss the tofu with the greens and add the sauce, stirring until the sauce thickens. Sprinkle with chili oil and cilantro; serve immediately.

Yield: 1 serving

Tofu Cabbage Stir-Fry

PREPARATION TIME: 15 to 20 minutes

Here is a fast meal for breakfast, lunch, or dinner on a cold winter day. The pressed tofu becomes golden brown and crispy in this stir-fry. If you don't have sesame seeds, go for it anyway.

1/3	block (4 to 5 ounces) firm tofu
1	teaspoon toasted sesame oil or vegetable oil
1	large clove garlic, minced
1	teaspoon minced fresh ginger
2	cups shredded green or red cabbage, (about 1/4 small head)
	Salt and pepper or soy sauce
1	teaspoon sesame seeds, toasted (see Note)

1. Sandwich the tofu between two plates. Top with a heavy book. Press for 15 to 20 minutes. Remove the weight and top cover, and drain the water from the bottom plate. The tofu is now ready to use. Cut the tofu into 1/2-inch cubes.

2. Heat 1/2 teaspoon of the oil in a nonstick skillet over medium-high heat. Add the tofu and stir and fry until lightly browned, 5 to 6 minutes. Add the garlic and ginger; sauté 1 minute longer. Remove the tofu from the skillet and set aside.

3. Re-oil the skillet with the remaining 1/2 teaspoon oil, and cook the cabbage over medium-high heat until soft, 3 to 5 minutes. Add the tofu. Remove the skillet from the heat. Season with salt and pepper or a splash of soy sauce. Serve when everything is hot. Sprinkle with toasted sesame seeds.

NOTE: To toast sesame seeds, place the seeds in a dry skillet on medium-high heat for 1 to 2 minutes. Stir the seeds and shake the pan frequently; when the seeds are golden, immediately remove them from the skillet. Watch the seeds carefully; they toast quickly.

Yield: 1 serving

Good Fortune Stir-Fry

PREPARATION TIME: 15 minutes

Have you ever wondered how Chinese restaurants get their stir-fries to glisten? The secret is in a sauce made with cornstarch. Choose one of the following sauce recipes and serve the stir-fry over a bed of cooked rice, pasta, or noodles.

Sweet and Sour Sauce

1	tablespoon soy sauce
1	tablespoon white vinegar
1	tablespoon catsup
2	teaspoons sugar
1/4	cup water
1	teaspoon cornstarch

Tangy Sauce

1	tablespoon hoisin sauce
1	tablespoon white vinegar
1	tablespoon soy sauce
1/4	cup water
1	teaspoon cornstarch

Stir-Fry

1	teaspoon vegetable oil
1	clove garlic, minced
1	medium carrot diagonally sliced (about 1 cup)
1/2	bell pepper, seeded and chopped, or 12 snow peas
1/2	medium zucchini, diagonally sliced (about 1 cup)
1	tablespoon finely chopped scallion (optional)

1. Choose one of the sauces and combine the sauce ingredients in a small bowl.

2. Heat the oil in a medium nonstick skillet over medium-high heat. Add the garlic and swirl it in the oil for a moment. Add the carrot, bell pepper, and zucchini; stir and fry for 3 to 4 minutes.

3. Stir the sauce and pour it over the vegetables; stir and simmer for about 30 seconds, or until the sauce thickens and the vegetables become glazed. Serve immediately. Garnish with chopped scallion if you desire.

Yield: 1 large serving

Pad Thai

PREPARATION TIME: 20 minutes

Making pad thai is easier than you might imagine. It's essentially a stir-fry with rice noodles. The recipe calls for mung bean sprouts. They are the sprouts you find in nearly every supermarket. The chile in this recipe is the ordinary little jalapeño pepper. If you like your food hot, leave in some of the seeds, but look out! The hardest part of this recipe is hand-grating 2 carrots. It takes about 4 minutes.

Noodles
2   quarts water
6   ounces rice noodles (1/4 inch wide)

Sauce
3   tablespoons fresh lemon or lime juice
3   tablespoons catsup
1   tablespoon sugar
1/4 cup soy sauce

Stir-Fry
1   to 2 tablespoons vegetable oil
4   large cloves garlic, minced
1   medium fresh green jalapeño, seeded and minced
2   medium carrots, grated (about 2 cups)
1/4 pound mung bean sprouts (about 1 1/2 cups)
4   scallions, finely chopped (about 3/4 cup)
2   tablespoons chopped peanuts
2   tablespoons finely chopped fresh cilantro or parsley (optional)

1. In a covered pan, bring the water to a rolling boil; stir in the rice noodles and cook for 5 to 7 minutes. Drain the noodles, rinse them well under cool water, and set aside.
2. In a small bowl, combine the sauce ingredients; set aside.
3. Heat the oil in a medium nonstick skillet on medium-high heat. Add the garlic and jalapeño pepper; stir and fry for a moment. Stir in the grated carrots. Stir and fry for 1 to 2 minutes. Add the sauce, noodles, bean sprouts, and scallions. Stir everything together. When the ingredients are warm, about 1 minute, remove to a platter. Garnish with the peanuts and cilantro if you desire.

NOTE: Just before you're ready to add the noodles to the carrot mixture, check to see if they're sticking together. If they are, quickly rinse and drain them again. They'll immediately come apart.

Yield: 2 very large or 3 medium servings

Broccoli, Carrot, and Cashew Stir-Fry

PREPARATION TIME: 10 minutes

Stir-fried fresh vegetables are one of the simplest and quickest meals you can make. Almost any combination of vegetables works. Figure on 2 to 2 1/2 cups of cut, raw vegetables per serving. If that seems like a lot, remember that vegetables shrink from water loss during cooking. If you can't find extra-firm tofu, firm will work.

3   ounces extra-firm tofu
2   teaspoons vegetable oil
1   clove garlic, finely chopped
1   carrot, diagonally sliced (1 cup)
1 1/2 cups broccoli florets
1   tablespoon soy sauce
2   tablespoons chopped scallion (1 small)
2   tablespoons coarsely chopped cashews

1. Blot the tofu between paper towels, then cut it into 1/2-inch cubes.

2. Heat the oil in a medium nonstick skillet on medium-high heat. Add the garlic and swirl it in the oil for 30 seconds; add the tofu, carrot, and broccoli. Stir and fry for about 3 minutes. Add the soy sauce; stir and fry for about 30 seconds.

3. Serve immediately. Garnish with the scallion and cashews.

Yield: 1 serving

Roasted Vegetable Rush

PREPARATION TIME: 12 minutes
COOKING TIME: 15 minutes

These brown and crispy potatoes take center stage, and the vegetables will be sweet and caramelized.

3	medium red potatoes (cut into 1-inch cubes)
3	mushrooms, quartered (about 1 cup)
3/4	green bell pepper, cut into bite-size chunks
5	cloves garlic, coarsely chopped
1	tablespoon olive oil
1	teaspoon dried rosemary
1	tablespoon fresh lemon juice or balsamic vinegar
	Salt and pepper

Preheat the broiler.

1. Cook the potato cubes in a pot of rapidly boiling water for 5 minutes. Drain thoroughly. Place the mushrooms, bell pepper, garlic, and cooked potatoes in a large bowl. Add the olive oil and rosemary, and stir to evenly coat the vegetables with oil.

2. Spread the vegetables onto a baking sheet; avoid building a thick layer; if piled high, the vegetables will steam not broil.

3. Broil vegetables for 10 minutes, until well-cooked but not burned. Stir once or twice to ensure even cooking. Serve the vegetables with a splash of fresh lemon juice or balsamic vinegar. Salt and pepper to taste.

Yield: 1 to 2 servings

Vegetable-Potato Combination

PREPARATION TIME: 10 minutes
COOKING TIME: 20 minutes

This meal turns heads in restaurants. It's the one you wish you had ordered. Make it at home for breakfast, lunch, or dinner.

1	teaspoon olive oil
2	to 3 medium potatoes cut into 1/2-inch chunks (about 2 cups)
1	carrot, chopped (about 1 cup)
1/2	medium green bell pepper, cut into 1/2-inch chunks (about 1/2 cup)
1/2	small onion, chopped (about 1/2 cup)
1/2	teaspoon dried dill
1/4	cup water
	Salt and pepper

1. Heat the oil in a medium nonstick skillet over medium-high heat. Add the potatoes, carrot, bell pepper, onion, and dill; sauté for 5 to 7 minutes stirring frequently.

2. Add the water. Reduce the heat to medium-low; cover and cook for 10 to 15 minutes, or until the potatoes are tender.

3. Remove the lid. If there is water in the pan, continue cooking for 1 to 2 minutes until the water evaporates. Salt and pepper to taste.

Yield: 2 servings

Basic Baked Potatoes

Eaten hot or cold, potatoes are easy to make for a simple snack or quick meal. You can steam them, bake them, boil them, mash them, pack them into soups and stews, fill them, dip them, and toss them into salads.

When baking potatoes, consider making several. Store the extras in the refrigerator When you're in a hurry, reheat one in a microwave for a quick meal or snack, or moisten the potato and reheat it in an oven at 350 degrees F for 15 minutes.

A baked potato can be a meal by itself. Make it a banquet by adding toppings. Top with sautéed or roasted vegetables, chili, spaghetti sauce, a ladle of soup, or a dollop of nonfat plain yogurt. Just don't do it all at the same time.

Preheat the oven to 350 to 400 degrees F.

1   or more russet potatoes
     Oil (optional)

Wash the potatoes, dry them, and rub with oil if you desire. Pierce the skin with a knife before baking. (Steam forms inside as they cook. They really *can* explode while baking.) Bake for about 60 minutes until fork-piercing tender.

Yield: 1 or more servings

Five-Minute
Microwave-Baked Potato

PREPARATION TIME: 1 minute
COOKING TIME: 5 minutes

If you are in a hurry and have a microwave, you can bake a potato in about 5 minutes.

1   potato

1. Wash and dry the potato and pierce it in several places.
2. Microwave on High for 5 minutes. Remove the potato from the microwave and let rest for 1 or 2 minutes. Squeeze the skin to see if the potato is soft. If it is, it's ready to eat. If it feels hard, return it to the microwave and heat on High for another minute. (It's better to undercook the potato, test for doneness, and return it to the microwave if necessary, than to overcook it. Overcooked microwaved potatoes shrivel and become pasty.) Because of the size of the potato and the power of the microwave, cooking times may vary.

NOTE: You can also microwave sweet potatoes and yams. Be sure to pierce the skin several times. A 6- to 8-ounce sweet potato will cook in 4 to 6 minutes on High power. Let it sit for 3 to 4 minutes before serving.

Yield: 1 serving

Mashed Potatoes

PREPARATION TIME: 6 minutes
COOKING TIME: About 15 minutes

Here is a real comfort food. If you can boil water, you can make this meal. If you like mashed potatoes with brown flecks, don't bother to peel them. One-third of the potato's nutrients are just beneath the skin. (The water used for cooking the potatoes can be the beginning of a great soup, provided that you have washed the potatoes before boiling them.) Do you like garlic? Add some when you mash the potatoes. Consider topping potatoes with grated cheese, sautéed vegetables, chopped cashews, or a handful of cooked corn or peas.

2	potatoes
2	to 3 tablespoons soy milk or nonfat dairy milk
	Salt and pepper

1. Cut the potatoes into thirds. Place the potatoes in a saucepan and cover them with water. Bring the pot to a boil; reduce the heat, cover, and simmer until tender, about 15 minutes.

2. Drain off the water. Mash the potatoes, mixing in the milk. Add more milk if the potatoes appear dry. Season with salt and pepper to taste.

Yield: 1 serving

Colcannon

This food favorite from Ireland and Scotland has only two main ingredients—potatoes and cabbage—and they're boiled together in one pot. It's a cheap, quick meal for a cold winter day. Save on dishwashing, and eat it out of the pot.

2 medium russet or white potatoes, peeled
2 cups shredded green cabbage
1/2 cup chopped onion (about 1/2 medium)
1/4 cup soy milk or lowfat dairy milk
1 to 2 tablespoons grated Cheddar cheese or soy cheese (optional)
   Salt and pepper

1. Cut the potatoes into 1-inch chunks. Place the potatoes in a medium pot, and cover them with water. Bring the water to a boil, and cook the potatoes until they are almost tender, about 10 minutes.

2. Add the cabbage and onion; continue cooking until the potatoes and cabbage are soft, about 5 minutes. Drain.

3. Add the milk and mash until the potatoes are smooth. Add cheese if you desire. Taste; season with salt and pepper. Enjoy!

Yield: 2 servings

Mashed Roots
with Horseradish

Preparation Time: 5 minutes
Cooking Time: About 20 minutes

*If you've wondered what to do with a turnip, here's one answer.
They're also good sliced and eaten raw. When you buy horseradish,
avoid brands made with egg yolk.*

2	red or white potatoes, cut into eighths
1	turnip, peeled and cut into eighths
1	carrot, cut into eighths
1	large clove garlic
2	to 4 tablespoons soy milk or dairy milk
	Salt and pepper
1	to 2 teaspoons horseradish
1	tablespoon minced fresh parsley (optional)

1. Place the potatoes, turnip, carrot, and garlic in a saucepan and cover with water. Bring the water to a boil; reduce the heat. Put a lid on the pot and simmer for about 20 minutes or until the vegetables are tender.

2. Drain the pot and add the milk. Mash and whip the mixture together until smooth. If necessary, add more milk. Season with salt and pepper. Taste, add horseradish, and stir. Serve sprinkled with parsley if you desire.

Yield: 2 servings

Scalloped Potatoes Vegan-Style

PREPARATION TIME: 15 minutes
COOKING TIME: About 1 hour

This recipe tastes like old-fashioned scalloped potatoes, but without the milk and cheese. If you don't have a lid for your baking dish, cover it with foil.

1	teaspoon olive oil
1	white onion, finely chopped
4	cloves garlic, minced
1/4	cup tahini
2	tablespoons whole wheat flour
1/2	teaspoon salt
1	cup water
5	medium white or red potatoes

Preheat the oven to 400 degrees F.

1. Heat the oil in a skillet and sauté the onion and garlic for 3 to 5 minutes on medium-high heat until the onion is soft and translucent.

2. In a blender or bowl, mix together the tahini, flour, salt, and water.

3. Thinly slice the potatoes. Don't bother to peel them. Arrange the potatoes in a lightly oiled 9-inch-square baking dish, overlapping them to cover the bottom of the dish. Spoon the onion and garlic mixture on top of the potato slices. Pour the tahini sauce over the top. Cover and bake for 1 hour. Uncover and bake another 5 to 10 minutes, until golden brown.

Yield: 2 servings

Sweet Potato or Yam with Raisins and Pineapple

PREPARATION TIME: 6 minutes
COOKING TIME: About 1 hour

Sweet potatoes and yams are good any time of the year. When cooked, they're almost sweet enough to eat for dessert. Serve this baked potato with cooked rice or couscous, and you'll have a filling meal. The cooked texture of the light-skinned variety sweet potato will be dry and crumbly. The dark-skinned variety, sometimes labeled yam, is sweeter and more moist inside. Both are delicious.

1	sweet potato or yam
1	teaspoon raisins
1/8	teaspoon ground cinnamon
4	tablespoons canned unsweetened crushed pineapple, drained
1	tablespoon chopped walnuts

Preheat the oven to 375 degrees F.

1. Place potato on a baking sheet, and bake for 1 hour or until tender. Remove the potato from the oven and peel away the shell, or cut the potato in half and scoop out the inside.

2. Mash the potato with a fork in a small bowl. Add raisins, cinnamon, pineapple, and walnuts. If the potato mixture is dry, add pineapple liquid. Top with walnuts.

Yield: 2 servings

CHAPTER 12

Desserts and Quick Breads

Here are sweet ideas for those times when you want to kick back and take a break. These cakes and quick breads can be popped in and out of the oven in a relatively short time. If you're having a chocolate attack, Dark Chocolate Pudding can be ready in 5 minutes, and Mountain High Chocolate Cake is made right in the baking pan so there's no mess to clean up. Brew a pot of strong coffee or hot tea and surprise your friends with warm Banana Bread.

Dark Chocolate Pudding

PREPARATION TIME: 5 minutes
COOKING TIME: 3 minutes

If you're not home alone, double the recipe and make a friend happy. (If you double the recipe, microwave on High for 3 minutes, stir, and microwave on High for another 2 minutes.)

2	tablespoons sugar
2	tablespoons unsweetened baking cocoa powder
2	teaspoons firmly packed cornstarch
3/4	cup soy milk or dairy milk
1/4	teaspoon vanilla

1. In a 1-quart glass microwavable bowl, combine the sugar, cocoa, and cornstarch. Add 1/4 cup of the milk and stir until mixture is smooth and creamy. Add the remaining 1/2 cup milk and stir.

2. Stir once just before you close the microwave door because cornstarch quickly settles to the bottom of the bowl. Microwave the milk mixture for 1 1/2 minutes on High. Remove the bowl from the microwave; stir carefully (the mixture will be hot). Return the pudding to the microwave, and cook for another 1 1/2 minutes on High. The pudding will begin to thicken.

3. Remove the bowl from the microwave, and add the vanilla. Stir once. Let the pudding rest for 1 to 2 minutes. It will continue to thicken as it cools.

NOTE: Microwave cooking times can vary depending on the size of the cooking container, the power supply, and the temperature settings available on the oven. If you don't have a microwave, you can make the pudding in a small saucepan on top of the stove. Combine the ingredients in the pot. Cook over medium heat, stirring constantly, until the pudding comes to a boil. Lower the heat and gently simmer, stirring continuously until the pudding thickens, about 3 minutes. It is important to keep stirring to avoid burning or scorching.

Yield: 1 serving

East Coast Custard

PREPARATION TIME: 12 minutes
COOKING TIME: About 1 1/2 hours

*Stir up this recipe after dinner, and you'll have a marvelous late
night snack. It turns into smooth pudding as it cooks slowly in the
oven. Serve it warm as is or topped with frozen vanilla yogurt.*

1/2   teaspoon vegetable oil
2/3   cup cornmeal
1/4   teaspoon salt
1   teaspoon chopped fresh ginger *or* 1/2 teaspoon ground
1/4   teaspoon nutmeg
2/3   cup raisins
4   cups soy milk or nonfat dairy milk
6   tablespoons maple syrup

Preheat the oven to 275 degrees F.

1. Lightly oil a 1 1/2- to 2-quart baking dish with vegetable oil.
   In a medium bowl, combine the cornmeal, salt, ginger, nutmeg, and raisins. Add 1 cup of the milk and the maple
   syrup. Stir to combine.

2. In a saucepan, heat 2 cups of milk to boiling. Gradually add
   the cornmeal mixture, stirring continuously. Reduce the
   heat to low and cook, stirring often, until the mixture is

thick and smooth, about 10 minutes. Transfer to the prepared baking dish.

3. Pour the remaining 1 cup of milk on top of the cornmeal mixture. Bake until the milk is nearly all absorbed and the top of the pudding is golden brown. Begin checking for doneness in 1 hour. The baking times can vary 15 to 30 minutes depending on the coarseness of the cornmeal. It will be soft and creamy inside when done.

Yield: 6 servings

Mountain High
Chocolate Cake

PREPARATION TIME: 7 minutes
BAKING TIME: 25 to 30 minutes

The best thing about this recipe is what it doesn't *have. It doesn't have eggs, milk, cholesterol, a mixing bowl to clean, or a pan to oil. It* does *deliver a delicious, dark chocolate cake. If you desire, serve the cake topped with a dollop of applesauce, and you'll have created a rustic version of the famous German Sacher torte.*

1 1/2 cups unbleached white flour
1/3 cup unsweetened baking cocoa powder
1 teaspoon baking soda
1/2 teaspoon salt
1 cup sugar
1 1/4 cups water
1/4 cup vegetable oil
2 teaspoons vanilla extract
2 tablespoons plain red or white vinegar

Preheat the oven to 375 degrees F.

1. In a baking pan (9-inch round, 8-inch square, or 9 × 6-inch rectangle), combine the flour, cocoa, baking soda, salt, and sugar.

2. In a small bowl, combine the water, oil, and vanilla. Pour the liquid into the dry ingredients, and whisk with a fork to combine. Add the vinegar, and stir just until the vinegar is distributed around the batter. (There will be color variations in the batter from the reaction between the vinegar and baking soda.)

3. Bake for 25 to 30 minutes. Remove from the oven, and call your friends.

Yield: 8 servings

Baked Apples

PREPARATION TIME: 6 minutes
BAKING TIME: About 35 minutes

Bake apples for dessert, and if you have leftovers, eat them for breakfast. For baking, Rome Beauty apples are the best, but Jonathan, Granny Smith, or Golden Delicious are also great. It's worth making this recipe for the baking aroma alone. Choose a filling or make one of each.

2   large Rome Beauty apples

Cinnamon-Raisin Filling
2   tablespoons brown sugar
2   tablespoons raisins
$1/2$ teaspoon ground cinnamon

Maple-Walnut Filling
2   tablespoons raisins
2   tablespoons maple syrup
1   tablespoon chopped walnuts

Preheat the oven to 400 degrees F.

1. With a knife, remove the core from each apple without cutting through the bottom. Make the hole large enough to accommodate the filling. Pare a $1 1/2$-inch strip of peel around the top of each apple.

216 Desserts and Quick Breads

2. Choose a filling, and combine ingredients. Fill the apples with the mixture.

3. Place the apples in a small baking pan and fill pan with $1/2$ inch of water. Bake until the apples are soft, about 35 minutes. Remove the apples from the oven. Cool slightly and serve.

Yield: 2 servings

Baked Bananas

PREPARATION TIME: 3 minutes
COOKING TIME: 10 to 15 minutes

Bananas will surprise you with how they change color while they bake. Warm and delicious, these bananas are a fast dessert when you're looking for something sweet to eat.

1   banana
1   to 2 tablespoons yogurt
1/8   teaspoon ground cinnamon

Preheat the oven to 400 degrees F.

1. Lay the unpeeled banana on a baking sheet. Make a slit along the length of the banana. Bake the banana with the slit side up for 10 to 15 minutes, or until the skin turns black.

2. Remove the banana from the oven, split open the peel, and eat it with a spoon. Top with a dollop of yogurt and a sprinkle of cinnamon.

Yield: 1 serving

Blueberry Cake

PREPARATION TIME: 6 minutes
COOKING TIME: 40 to 45 minutes

Everyone loves blueberries. Serve this cake with a cup of strong coffee or a hot cup of tea, and take a break.

1 1/2 cups flour
1/2   cup sugar
2   teaspoons baking powder
1/4   teaspoon salt
1   cup soy milk or lowfat dairy milk
1/4   cup vegetable oil
1   cup fresh or frozen blueberries, rinsed or thawed and drained

Preheat the oven to 350 degrees F.

1. In a medium bowl, combine the flour, sugar, baking powder, and salt. Add the milk and oil; mix until the batter is smooth. Pour the mixture into a lightly oiled 6 × 9-inch baking pan.

2. Sprinkle the berries on top.

3. Bake for 40 to 45 minutes, or until the top is golden.

Yield: 6 to 8 servings

Banana Bread

PREPARATION TIME: 15 minutes
COOKING TIME: About 45 minutes
COOLING TIME: at least 15 minutes

*Here is a wonderful way to use up very ripe bananas and make
your friends happy at the same time. This bread gets its crunch
from Grape-Nuts cereal instead of nuts. Use a potato masher or
a strong fork to squish the bananas.*

1 1/2   cups flour (3/4 cup white + 3/4 cup whole wheat, *or*
        1 1/2 cups white)
3/4   cup Grape-Nuts cereal
1/3   cup sugar
1/2   cup raisins
1   teaspoon baking powder
1/4   teaspoon baking soda
1/4   teaspoon salt (optional)
2   egg whites
1   cup mashed very ripe banana (2 to 3 medium)
1/2   cup plain nonfat yogurt
1/4   cup vegetable oil
2   teaspoons vanilla or 1/2 teaspoon ground cinnamon

Preheat the oven to 350 degrees F.

1. In a large bowl, combine the flour, Grape-Nuts, sugar,
   raisins, baking powder, baking soda, and salt.

2. In another bowl, beat the egg whites until they are frothy, and combine them with the mashed bananas, yogurt, oil, and vanilla. Add the banana mixture to the dry ingredients, stirring the two until the dry ingredients are just moistened.

3. Lightly oil an $8^1/_2 \times 4^1/_2 \times 3$-inch loaf pan with vegetable oil. Pour in the batter. Bake the bread for 40 to 45 minutes or until a wooden toothpick inserted into the center comes out clean. Let the bread cool in the pan for about 15 minutes, then turn it out to finish cooling. Enjoy!

Yield: 8 servings

Corn Bread

PREPARATION TIME: 7 minutes
COOKING TIME: 20 to 25 minutes

This tasty corn bread is an excellent accompaniment to a bowl of chili, soup, or salad.

1 1/3   cups unbleached white flour
2/3   cup yellow cornmeal
2   tablespoons sugar
2   teaspoons baking powder
1/4   teaspoon salt
1   cup soy milk or dairy milk
3   tablespoons vegetable oil
2   egg whites
      Honey or fruit preserves (optional)

Preheat the oven to 425 degrees F.

1. Lightly oil a 9 × 5-inch baking dish or loaf pan with vegetable oil. In a large bowl, combine the flour, cornmeal, sugar, baking powder, and salt.

2. In a medium bowl, combine the milk, vegetable oil, and egg whites.

3. Pour the liquid mixture into the dry ingredients and stir just to combine. Do not overmix. Pour the mixture into the baking pan. Bake for 20 to 25 minutes. Serve warm with honey or fruit preserves, if you desire.

Yield: 6 big slices

Sunday Morning Muffins

PREPARATION TIME: 10 minutes
COOKING TIME: 18 to 20 minutes

Set out a jar of honey or jam and enjoy these muffins straight from the oven. The trick to making high-rising, tender muffins is in the blending. Too much stirring makes them tough. When you combine the flour mixture with the applesauce mixture, stir only until the dry ingredients become moist. If a few lumps remain, that's okay.

1	cup whole wheat flour
1	cup white flour
1/4	cup sugar
2	teaspoons baking powder
3/4	teaspoon baking soda
1/2	teaspoon ground cinnamon
3/4	cup raisins
2	cups unsweetened applesauce
1/4	cup vegetable oil

Preheat the oven to 375 degrees F.

1. In a large bowl, combine the flours, sugar, baking powder, baking soda, cinnamon, and raisins, stirring well to evenly combine the dry ingredients.

2. In a medium bowl, whisk the applesauce and oil together.

3. Add the applesauce mixture to the flour mixture stirring just to moisten. Spoon the batter into a lightly oiled standard muffin tin. Bake for 18 to 20 minutes, or until golden.

Yield: 12 muffins

CHAPTER 13

Make Life Easy, Take a Coffee Break

The first coffee drinkers of the Arab world used coffee not as a beverage, but as a drug to help them stay awake and alert during their long evening prayers. If coffee has become an integral part of your life during long nights of studying, here are some ideas to help you use it to your best advantage.

Although coffee isn't a health food, research done in the last few years has turned up very little scientific evidence to indict most coffee drinkers. A moderate intake of two cups daily does not pose a serious or even minor health threat. Similar to amphetamines but milder in its effects, caffeine stimulates the sympathetic nervous system, which regulates the body's automatic functions. As a central nervous system stimulant, it makes people feel more alert, temporarily relieves fatigue, and promotes quick thinking. It doesn't take much caffeine to accomplish this feeling of well-being. The amount in one or two ordinary cups of coffee is enough. However, at greater doses (five to six cups or more), caffeine can produce negative effects such as nervousness, anxiety, and panic attacks. Caffeine is also present in black and green teas and some soft drinks.

There are coffee alternatives without caffeine made from roasted grains, roots, and seeds that instantly dissolve in hot water to create a coffee-like beverage. The stronger you make the brew, the more it resembles coffee. Although interesting in their own right, these substitutes are not for fanatical coffee drinkers.

Prepared coffee doesn't keep well. Warming it over a burner for only about 20 minutes can make the taste bitter. If you are making coffee for only one person, the filter method is a good choice. It's simple to make only one or two cups at a time and clean up is easy. Measure 2 rounded tablespoons of ground coffee per cup into a filter-lined cone poised over your pot or cup. (In the world of coffee, a cup is 6 ounces not the 8 ounces in a standard measuring cup. So if you are using a measuring cup or a giant coffee mug to measure water, your coffee will probably be weak.) Rinse the pot and cup with hot water before you make the coffee, and the drink will remain hot longer. Heat cold fresh water just until it boils. Remove the water from the heat. Next, add just a few splashes of water to the coffee grounds to moisten them slightly. Let them absorb the water before pouring on the rest. This will prevent the water from going through the grounds too quickly without extracting maximum flavor.

If you plan to make your coffee by the pot, the plunger-pot method is the favored brewing technique. Simply pour hot water over coarsely ground coffee and allow it to steep for a few minutes. A stainless mesh filter is "plunged" down to the bottom, neatly separating the coffee from the grounds. The brew is rich, thick, and flavorful.

Coffee grounds make great compost. Add them to your houseplants' soil for excellent results.

Coffee Brazil

1   cup coffee
1   sliver lemon peel

Pour hot coffee into a cup. Twist the lemon peel to release its oils. Rub the yellow side of the peel around the rim of the cup for a citrus-flavored coffee.

Yield: 1 serving

Café au Lait

This foamy mixture satisfies first thing in the morning or late at night. You will need a blender to foam the milk. It won't reach the heights of the steamed milk from an espresso bar, but it won't cost as much either.

$1/2$ cup soy milk or dairy milk
1   teaspoon honey
$1/2$ cup freshly brewed strong coffee

Heat the milk and honey to a boil, then whip it in a blender for 30 seconds. Next, pour the coffee into a cup and add the milk.

Yield: 1 serving

Coffee Alaska

1   cup hot, freshly brewed coffee

$1/4$ cup soy ice cream, nonfat frozen yogurt, or dairy ice cream

Pour the coffee over vanilla or chocolate ice cream or frozen yogurt. If you drink the coffee quickly enough—before all the ice cream melts—you'll have a delicious warm puddle to sip from the bottom of your cup.

Yield: 1 serving

Banana Coffee Cooler

You will need a blender for this recipe.

$1/2$ ripe banana
$1/2$ cup strong coffee
$1/4$ pint coffee-flavored frozen yogurt or soy or
      dairy ice cream
$1/2$ teaspoon vanilla

Cut up the banana and put it into the blender. Add the remaining ingredients and blend until smooth and creamy.

Yield: 1 serving

Mocha Coffee

Make this delicious coffee with equal parts hot coffee and hot chocolate.

¹/₂   cup hot coffee
¹/₂   cup hot chocolate
       Grated orange peel

1. Stir the coffee and hot chocolate together. Serve topped with grated orange peel.

Yield: 1 serving

CHAPTER 14

Beer and Vegetarianism

Jeff Byles

Beer and college are closely, and often notoriously, paired in popular imagination.

Movies like *Animal House* and *Revenge of the Nerds* stereotype college beer drinkers as brew-guzzling, hard-partying maniacs. Strange collegiate traditions routinely involve emptying beer kegs. Scenes of brew-induced mayhem around campus are, unfortunately, all too common in the real world. Beer's reputation has accordingly suffered.

The recent renaissance in microbrewing shows that beer has a tradition all its own. Microbrewers have revived centuries-old brewing traditions, making their beer in small batches with care and pride. A few years ago there were just a few brands of beer, today there are literally hundreds.

"Craft-brewed" beer has restored the dignity, quality, and pleasure to a pint of frothy ale or lager. Starting with fresh malted barley, seasoning the brew with extravagantly floral hop flowers, and fermenting with authentic yeast strains, craft brewers prize their ingredients much as vegetarians might prize a perfectly ripe avocado.

Actually beer and vegetarianism have a lot in common. When people encounter a vegetarian, they often ask incredulously, "But, what do you eat?" It is as if the world of food without meat amounted to a few heads of wilted iceberg lettuce and a pitiable stalk of broccoli.

As any vegetarian knows, a little patient experimentation yields delicious meat-free rewards. What plump roast could ever compare with a tangy, succulent dish of pad thai?

Similarly, many beer consumers find it hard to believe that there is a vast world of beer beyond the pale-hued, mass-produced beers like Budweiser, Coors, and Miller. While those beers are not necessarily bad, drinking a mass-market "light" beer is like eating packaged macaroni and cheese when you could just as easily be dining on an elegant dish of Pasta al Pesto.

Like vegetarian cuisine, the world of beer is bursting with flavor. Try whatever comes your way: a nicely balanced pale ale, crisp with hops; a dark and roasty stout, thick and velvety as a milk shake; or real Belgian ale, tart and sweet with a delicately soft maltiness.

Besides increasing your gustatory pleasure, exploring beer is a way of educating your palate—much like exploring the unfamiliar territory of painting is how one learns to appreciate art.

This is not to say that there aren't other, more practical uses for beer. There are a variety of resourceful ways the steepings of malts can improve human morale. Should you find yourself in the possession of a quantity of beer that is, for whatever reasons, undrinkable, do not despair.

According to naturopaths, beer makes a wonderful shampoo, hydrating the hair while adding protein from the grains. Many home brewers claim that beer serves tolerably well as an insect barrier, and they dispense it liberally around their garden. Some other, perhaps unorthodox, uses for our wonderfully versatile malt beverage are as follows:

- Keep it in a sacred vessel and use sparingly for rituals honoring Ninkasi, the goddess of brewing.

- Freeze it for use in "beer-sicles."
- Age it carefully for a few months in a sealed container to make malt vinegar.
- Boil off most of the liquid to obtain "essence of beer," creating a captivating new perfume and cologne.

When William Blake wrote that the road of excess leads to the palace of wisdom, I do not believe he was talking about beer. Should you happen to venture that way, however, there are a few things to know about how beer affects the body. While cures for hangovers are prolific, beware, they are mostly the stuff of myth.

The liver needs only two essential aids to process the alcohol in beer—plenty of time and water. Because alcohol is a strong diuretic, it causes the body to lose water. Therefore drinking water before and while you drink alcohol will help avoid that morning headache. Food also slows the rate of alcohol absorption from the stomach, so having a plate of falafel with a pitcher of ale will help ease the effects of alcohol on the body.

Researchers have found that women need to be particularly careful when drinking, because women's alcohol tolerance varies at different times of the month. A premenstrual woman will be most vulnerable to alcohol, because during this time enzyme action in the liver slows, causing more alcohol to accumulate in the bloodstream.

Beer can indeed be a profound part of anyone's education. Rich in tradition, robust in culture, and mellifluous in taste, beer offers a wealth of meaning unlike any other beverage. That luminous pint of ale can incite the intellect and soothe the soul.

Now that's beer for thought.

Resources

Suggested Reading

Jackson, Michael. *Michael Jackson's Beer Companion*. Philadelphia: Running Press, 1993. (An informative survey of world beers arranged by style. Jackson, recognized as the world's most distinguished beer writer, weaves brewing history together with detail about specific breweries and beers.)

Living Planet. *The Animal Rights Handbook—Everyday Ways to Save Animal Lives*. Washington, D.C.: Living Planet Press, 1990.

Robbins, John. *Diet for a New America*. Walpole, NM: Stillpoint Publishing International, Inc., 1987.

Environmental Organizations

EarthSave International
620 B Distillery Commons
Louisville, KY 40206-9849
(502) 589-7676 General Information
(800) 362-3648 Membership and Book Orders Only
Web site: http://www.earthsave.org

EarthSave promotes the benefits of plant-based food choices for our health, our environment, and a more compassionate world. Call or write for information on volunteer opportunities, educational materials, or questions about EarthSave's new projects.

Youth for Environmental Sanity (YES)
420 Bronco Road
Soquel, CA 95073
(408) 465-1081
E-mail: kamps@yesworld.org

Animal Rights Groups

Farm Animal Reform Movement (FARM)
P.O. Box 30654
Bethesda, MD 20824
E-mail: farmusa@erols.com
Web site: http://envirolink.org/arrs/farm

People for the Ethical Treatment of Animals (PETA)
501 Front Street
Norfolk, VA 23510
(757) 622-7382

Vegetarian Groups

North American Vegetarian Society
P.O. Box 72
Dolgeville, NY 13329
(518) 568-7970

Vegetarian Resource Group
P.O. Box 1463
Baltimore, MD 21203
(410) 366-VEGE or (410) 366-8343

Index

French toast
  2000, 28
  banana, 31
Fresh salsa, 42
Fruits
  salad, 70
  yogurt shake with, 40

G

Garbanzo beans. *See also*
  Hummus
  pasta with, 174–175
  rice with, 159
Garlic
  about, 10
  bread with attitude, 107
  dressing, creamy, 89
  eggplant spread with, 47
  preparation, 23
  roasted, spread, 46
Ginger
  about, 10
  green stir-fry, Chinese,
    190–191
Gingered Chinese greens
  stir-fry, 190–191
Gingerroot, preparation, 23
Good fortune stir-fry,
  194–195
Grains. *See also specific types*
  about, 143–144
  cooking chart, 147
  preparation, 144–147
Grapefruit, about, 10
Grapes, about, 10
Grating, about, 20
Gravy, mushroom, polenta
  with, 150–151
Greek-style scrambled
  tofu, 35

Green beans, feta cheese pasta
  with, 166–167
Green chile quesadilla, 109
Greens. *See also specific types*
  bean crostini with, 103–104
  pasta with, 176–177
  preparation, 23
  rice and yams with, 160–161
Green salad with oranges, 72
Guacamole–the real thing, 45

H

Honey-yogurt dressing, 88
Horseradish, mashed roots
  with, 205
Hot cakes. *See* Pancakes
Hot lips fajita, 116
Hot oats and raisins, 32
Hummus, 48

I

Impulse minestrone
  soup, 52–53
Indian rice, 154
Italian squash. *See* Zucchini

K

Kale
  about, 11
  potato soup with, 62
  vegetable medley, 64–65
Kiwi, about, 11

L

Leeks
  about, 11
  preparation, 24

Lemons
about, 11
preparation, 24
Lentils
dal, 134–135
soup, 60–61
Lettuce, about, 11
Limes, about, 11

M

Marinated tempeh, 140–141
Marinated vegetables, 76–77
Mashed potatoes, 203
Mashed roots, horseradish
with, 205
*Michael Jackson's Beer
Companion*, 237
Microbrewing
vegetarianism and,
233–235
Microwaving, about, 21
Mince, about, 20
Miso-happy soup, 50–51
Mocha coffee, 231
Moroccan stew, 66
Mountain high chocolate cake,
214–215
Muffins, Sunday
morning, 223
Mung bean sprouts,
about, 13
Mushrooms
about, 11–12
barley soup with, 56–57
burger, cremini, 94–95
gravy, polenta with,
150–151
pepper pita pizza with, 120
preparation, 24
Mustard, sweet, vinaigrette, 90

N

Noodles. *See* Rice noodles
North American Vegetarian
Society, 238
Nuts
cashew, broccoli, and carrot
stir-fry, 198
peanut pasta, 179–180

O

Oatmeal
about, 144
overnight, 33
preparation, 145
raisins and, hot, 32
One potato, two potato
salad, 69
Onions
about, 12
preparation, 24
Oranges
about, 12
green salad with, 72
pineapple yogurt
salad, 81
rice, black bean salad
with, 79
Overnight oatmeal, 33

P

Pad thai, 196–197
Pancakes
beer, 30
fluffy vegan, 29
polenta, 36
spaghetti, 178
Pans, 18
Parsnips, about, 12

Q

Quesadillas
  black bean and yam,
    110–111
  green chile, 109
  zucchini, spicy, 114

R

Raisins
  apple couscous with, 73
  oatmeal and, hot, 32
  yams and pineapple
    with, 208
Ramen noodles, 164
Red peppers, roasted,
  188–189
Revenge of the Nerds, 233
Rice
  about, 144
  brown. *See* Brown rice
  fried, Chinese, 155
  garbanzo beans with, 159
  Indian, 154
  orange, black bean salad
    with, 79
  preparation, 146–147
  Sicilian, 158
  Vera Cruz, 162
Rice noodles
  about, 164
  pad thai, 196–197
Rice pudding cereal, 37
Roasted red bell peppers,
  188–189
Roasted vegetable pizza, 121
Roasted vegetable rush, 199
Roasting, about, 20
Rolled oats. *See* Oatmeal
Rutabagas, about, 14

S

Salads. *See also* Dressings
  about, 67
  avocado and pear, 85
  bean, buttery, 78
  cabbage slaw, 71
  downtown, 84
  fruit, 70
  green, with oranges, 72
  orange rice and black bean
    salad, 79
  pasta, 68
  pineapple-orange
    yogurt, 81
  potato, 69
  tabbouleh, traditional,
    74–75
  taco, 82–83
  white bean and tomato, 80
Salsa, fresh, 42
Sandwiches
  about, 91
  beyond beef, 93
  chapati with confetti
    salad, 92
  creamy zucchini, pita, 106
  curry in a hurry, 99
  eggplant, broiled,
    100–101
  falafel, 96–97
  zucchini Parmesan
    broiled, 98
Sauces
  tahini dipping, 44
  tsiziki, 43
Sautéing, about, 21
Scalloped potatoes vegan-style,
  206–207
Scrambled tofu curry, 34
Seasoning, 25–26

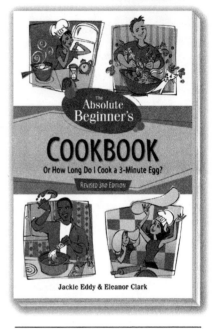

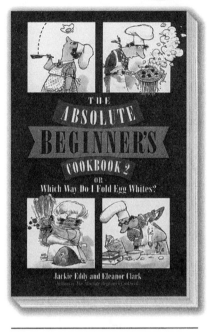